Teaching Children's Literature in the Primary School

Dedication

For Malindi Louise Fenwick: and for Tom and Mina Fenwick, in whose home I became literate.

Teaching Children's Literature in the Primary School

Geoff Fenwick

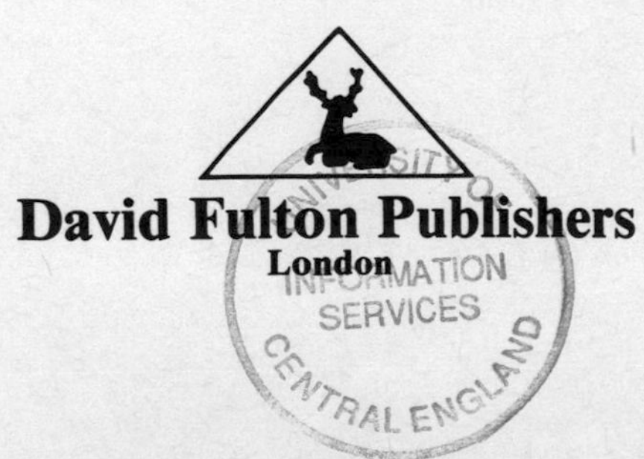

David Fulton Publishers
London

David Fulton Publishers Ltd
2 Barbon Close, Great Ormond Street, London WC1N 3JX

First published in Great Britain by
David Fulton Publishers 1990

British Library Cataloguing in Publication Data

Fenwick, Geoff
Teaching children's literature in the primary school.
1. Primary schools. Curriculum subjects: English literature. Teaching
I. Title
372.64

ISBN 1-85346-121-0

Typeset by Chapterhouse, Formby L37 3PX
Printed in Great Britain by BPCC Wheatons Ltd, Exeter

Acknowledgements

My understanding of Children's Literature and how it might be taught has been influenced during the past twenty years by:

Harry Basson, Terry O'Brien, Geoff Evans and the late Norman Garner of the Ethel Wormald College of Education, Liverpool.

Elizabeth Bradburn and John Vaughan of Liverpool University

Jeanette Coltham and David Preen of the University of Manchester

Cedric Cullingford of Charlotte Mason College of Education

Geoff Fox of Exeter University

William Murray and John Mowat of the University of Lancaster

Thanks are also due to the many teachers with whom I have worked on in-service courses, particularly those involved with the DASE course in Children's Literature from the time of its origin in 1976 to the present day: and to Dee Reid and Ken Hills for their help and advice during the time that this book was being written.

Extracts from Laurie Lee's I Can't Stay Long are quoted with the permission of André Deutsch Ltd. Every effort has been made to trace the ownership of the copyright material in this book. It is the publishers' belief that the necessary permissions from publishers, authors, and authorised agents have been obtained, but in the event of any question arising as to the use of any material, the publishers, while expressing regret for any error unconsciously made, will be pleased to make the necessary corrections in future editions of this book.

Geoff Fenwick
March 1990

The Author

Geoff Fenwick trained as a teacher at the City of Leeds College and later gained an Advanced Diploma at Liverpool University and an M.Ed. degree at the University of Manchester. He taught in primary schools in Leeds, Uganda and Lancashire and was a deputy head for three years. He then became a lecturer in education at the Ethel Wormald College, Liverpool, and now occupies a similar position in the School of Education and Community Studies at Liverpool Polytechnic. He works with qualified teachers studying on a D.A.S.E. course in Children's Literature of which he is the director and with undergraduates working for awards in education and librarianship. His research interests include creative writing, sustained reading and story telling and he has published many articles in journals and the educational press. Geoff Fenwick still works regularly with children.

Contents

Introduction

This book is intended mainly for teachers in training and for those at the start of their teaching careers. As they become familiar with the requirements of the National Curriculum it will become obvious to them that Children's Literature is at the very centre of language teaching in primary schools. They will have to know what stories to read and tell to their pupils and how to do this effectively. They will require an understanding of children's reading habits and how responses to literature can be developed. And they will need to have a working knowledge of the reading material which is available. Such expertise is needed right across the primary age range. Although the emphasis might be different, it is as important to teachers of infant children as it is to their colleagues in junior departments.

The ideas and experiences brought together in this book represent the collective wisdom of many teachers in schools and in higher education. Wherever possible, sources have been acknowledged. Some readers will, no doubt, recognise ideas which they have encountered elsewhere. This is inevitable when the major factors essential to the teaching of children's literature in the primary school are collected together within the pages of a single book.

It would be misleading and unfair, however, to pretend that the chapters which follow are devoid of originality. For many years I have been fortunate to work with a large number of teachers on in-service courses during which useful ideas about story-telling, sustained reading and the use of alternative literature have been developed. Some of them, controversial at the time of their inception, are now considered to be good practice. Others are still under investigation and include the use of local folktales, the encouragement of spoken poetry and the ways by which teachers might sift through the large number of children's books which are available to them at the present time. In this respect, this book need not be confined to teachers at the start of their careers. I would like to think that the ideas developed alongside experienced teachers will be useful to some of their contemporaries at least, particularly to those who have not been able to investigate the field in any depth.

There has probably never been a better time to write a book about Children's Literature. More children's books are being published than ever before, most of them are well produced: many are finding their way into schools. New writers are adding to the already rich variety of our literary heritage. Even poetry, long neglected, is becoming more popular.

Yet the presence of books in school is not, in itself, enough. To be really effective, Children's Literature must not only be available, it has to be taught. Too many children who are competent readers do not particularly like reading. If they lack enthusiasm in the primary school they are unlikely to become committed readers when they move on to secondary education. Indeed, it has been estimated that at least one third of all secondary pupils over 14 read very few books. There is also the danger that when compared to the shiny new technology which is present in increasing quantities in primary schools, even the most attractive books might appear to be old fashioned or even obsolete.

Can Children's Literature be taught? Many young teachers will have reservations about this. What they probably fear is that such teaching might require so much formality and uniformity that most of the enjoyment which can be derived from working with fiction might be lost. This view tends to equate literature teaching at primary level with the examination work which takes place at the top end of the secondary school. The examination of literature has in the past been not particularly successful although recent approaches have been more useful.

Literature is taught well in many primary schools. Every teacher who knows what to read to children, and how to read it, is teaching literature. Every school which has a comprehensive stock of books, both old and new, that are used frequently by children is assisting the process. When there is adequate time to read books and when strategies which develop children's responses to them are in use, then teaching Children's Literature really starts to take off. Even the shiny new technology need create few problems. For literature has its own technology. This should not be neglected. Videos, cassettes and television programmes can, like comics and magazines, assist in the teaching of literature rather than rival it.

Above all, Children's Literature needs to be taught with

enthusiasm. It will only excite and attract pupils if it does the same for their teachers. Many teachers possess this enthusiasm. Ironically, they might well be the ones who are most worried about what lies ahead. It is not so much the content of the National Curriculum which causes anxiety. Indeed, in terms of Children's Literature it incorporates much that is forward looking and exciting. It is the testing which is worrying. Despite the claims that externally imposed tests will take precedence over classroom evaluations it is my belief that eventually a great deal will depend upon the latter which will often be what teachers are already doing. The National Curriculum is not fixed. Like earlier reforms it will contain some ideas which are impracticable and even dotty as well as much which is useful. As it settles down the testing of Children's Literature will, I think, become economical in terms of time and will depend very much upon the sort of recording which should be going on anyway. If we are aware of what our pupils read and the ways in which they link this reading with talking, listening and writing then the National Curriculum need not be formidable. Above all, the National Curriculum should be seen as a two-way process: it informs teachers but it is also informed by them.

Why do we teach Children's Literature anyway? There are a number of convincing reasons. We should teach it, for instance, because it can help to improve children's reading. Equally important, it can help to improve their attitudes to reading. And by studying literature it is certainly possible for children to become more effective writers. Then there is the social factor. The majority of teachers who have much to do with either adult or juvenile fiction are probably aware of its civilising potential. Used sensitively, literature can help children to come to terms with the real world. It can also allow them to fantasise in a harmless way. It can even be a form of escapism and, provided it is not overdone, there is little harm in that.

The socialising influence of literature is probably at its best in schools where reading is a shared experience within groups both large and small. That is why telling and reading stories to children are such important activities. No one should underestimate the power of story.

Teaching literature should help pupils to enjoy books. This is not merely stating the obvious. Faulty, mistaken approaches can cause children to dislike reading. At crucial times, for example when a reading scheme has just been completed, it takes no more than three or four unsuccessful experiences with books to convince some children that reading is neither interesting nor pleasurable. Conversely, if a child is fascinated by a book, complex vocabulary and a complicated plot are not necessarily formidable barriers.

We can also teach literature because it is there. It is part of our heritage which is passed down from one generation to the next. Whether we like it or not, *Dennis the Menace* belongs to it as much as *Alice in Wonderland*, *Black Beauty* or *Treasure Island*. It is a dynamic process. Books, magazines and comics become dated and obsolete or else stand the test of time and go on to be accepted as classic fiction. The literature available to us will always be a mixture of contemporary work and what has survived from the past. This heritage should not have narrow confines. Classical myths, folk tales from other countries and children's fiction from overseas should all be included provided that they have relevance.

I hope that the readers of this book will enjoy it and find it useful. Teaching Children's Literature has been a source of great joy to me in both primary schools and higher education. As I near the end of one career another, as a writer and story teller, seems to be just beginning.

Note: The National Curriculum

The implications of the National Curriculum for each topic in this book will be considered at the end of each chapter. As story in terms of classroom practice is being dealt with in Chapter 2 it seems appropriate to discuss the links with the National Curriculum there.

It is useful, however, to consider how the documents will be used.

(1) The programmes of study provide details of the content which is to be taught. Material from the programmes for Speaking and Listening, Reading and Writing will all be considered.

(2) The Attainment targets specify what children should achieve. Again, Speaking and Listening, Reading and Writing will be dealt with.

(3) Non-statutory guidance provides information and suggestions for planning and the devising of schemes of work. Once more, the three elements mentioned above will be taken into account.

At the present time, only Key Stage 1 is statutory. Key Stage 2 is also discussed although the documents relating to it are not yet finalised.

CHAPTER 1

The Power of Story

The bed-time story: a four-year old listens to a traditional tale she has heard many times before. Its familiarity comforts her yet she is still thrilled by its excitement. She can remember it, almost word for word. If a single sentence is omitted the reader is speedily reminded.

The poetry reading: a famous poet prepares to read his best known work to a live audience. There is an expectant hush.

The club: an experienced comedian works his way through his act. Each joke is timed to perfection. There is no clinking of glasses, no conversations: only the comedian's voice and the bursts of laughter when each joke reaches its climax.

'Are you sitting comfortably? Then I'll begin.' 'Listen with Mother' – a radio programme long since abandoned – captivated pre-school children with simple, well told stories.

'What will happen to Dick, Jock and Snowy? Will the time bomb explode? Listen to the next instalment of Dick Barton, Special Agent.' In the early 1950s this programme ensured that little homework was done until the nightly episode was complete.

The classroom: *A Tale of Two Cities* is being serialised. Today's instalment is concluded as Sidney Carton takes the place of his friend in the condemned cell. Three children rush out to the teacher's desk to ask what happens next.

The cinema: the serial ends with the hero tied to a post while the fuse of the gun-powder barrel burns short. Next Saturday most of the young audience will return to find out the results.

The courtroom: the eminent laywer is persuading the jury that her client is entirely innocent. All eyes are on her.

The common denominator of these apparently disparate incidents is story. Story is a common yet dramatic form of communication. Its power has fascinated philosophers, writers, psychologists, librarians, folk-lorists, teachers and librarians, and of course, countless audiences large and small. It is perhaps the most versatile form of communication in existence. Its audience can be a single person or a thousand. It can be as effective on the screen as it is when the performance is live.

Story-telling might not be as old as the hills but it is certainly almost as old as the human race. There is not a country in the world which does not possess its own unique collection of folk tales, myths and legends. In the ancient city of Marrakesh the story-tellers use the same stories as their forefathers did. Australian aborigines not only paint symbolic story pictures but carve them onto their boomerangs as well. All this, you might think, is a far cry from 'Jackanory' and yet, wherever and however stories are told, the shared human experience is the same.

The psychologist Bruno Bettelheim and the educator Harold Rosen, both distinguished in their respective fields, have constantly pointed out the effectiveness of story. Teachers have an important part to play in developing their ideas. Their role is different from that of parent for their audience is usually much larger. Ideally, a teacher's work should complement that already done at home.

Teachers who tell stories are doing more than passing on culture: they are teaching in an interesting way. If they tell stories well, they are providing useful models of communication for their pupils. The child who listens to a good story-teller is likely to become competent in the art too. This will be reflected not only in oral work but in a child's writing. A pupil who can tell a good story is likely, sooner or later, to write a good story too. By telling stories a whole pattern is established.

Anne Pellowski, who seems to have tracked down story-telling past and present in almost every part of the globe, describes its rich variety in Western Europe, in the Middle Ages. Strolling players, praise singers, bards and minstrels all provided stories in one form or another. Often story-telling was much more than a pastime: for some, it was a profession. Sometimes the job was hereditary. Often it required a lengthy apprenticeship. Chief bards, the Poets Laureate of their times, needed a repertoire of 350 stories. In some societies it was the story-tellers who carried the oral history of people in their heads. In parts of Africa this still happens today.

Oral history is essential in pre-literate societies. Once a language becomes written as well as spoken then the art of story-telling becomes sub-divided into two separate but similar activities: story-telling and story-reading. Often the two are confused. As the table indicates, there are marked differences.

Clearly, the ancient art of story-telling is not necessarily book based. Without the encumbrance of a book to hold and read from it is possible to have almost constant eye contact with the audience. The

Story telling	Story reading
Oral and written sources	Written sources only
Committed to memory	Not committed to memory
Very frequent eye contact with the audience	A limited amount of eye contact with the audience
A dramatic style of presentation is easy	A dramatic style of presentation is difficult
Stories are usually short	Stories can be both long and short
Prolonged serialisation is difficult	Prolonged serialisation is fairly easy
Audience participation is easy	Audience participation is limited

absence of a book also means that dramatic presentation is much more easy; there is more freedom to move about and to use a variety of gestures and other non-verbal signals. Yet because a told story has to be memorised it is not very easy to serialise.

Justifying the use of stories

Teachers who read and tell stories will readily agree that both activities are valuable. The primary school in which I was educated had a copy of the well-known painting 'The boyhood of Raleigh' on its walls. The portrait of the Elizabethan sailor sitting on the shore and pointing out to sea while he spun out his yarn to his rapt young audience has for many years epitomised for me the spirit of telling stories. Just occasionally, in my travels around schools, I still see a copy.

Teachers of young children instinctively sense that the child who comes to school with the experience of many tales already told or read at home has a headstart in language development. It simply makes sense to continue with this good work or, in the case of less fortunate children, to commence it. Unfortunately, surveys seem to indicate that story-telling becomes much less frequent once children leave their infant departments. Story-reading does not fare so badly but there seems to be an implication that by the time a child can read with some degree of independence both activities become obsolete. Yet how can we agree with this supposition if we accept that both activities:

- develop listening skills;
- improve and increase vocabulary;

- increase reading competence;
- improve written and oral work;
- increase sensitivity;
- encourage imagination;
- develop positive attitudes towards books and reading;
- introduce children to a rich variety of literature;
- encourage children's interest in fantasy;
- assist children to come to terms with real life situations;
- make them aware of their own and others' cultural heritage;
- present children with a valuable shared experience?

It becomes clear that the necessity to tell and read stories *throughout* the primary school is reinforced.

One distinguished educator has become so convinced of the power of story-telling that he has advocated it as the basis for every lesson taught in schools. We will return to Egan's ideas in Chapter 2. At the very least they indicate that story-telling and story-reading are being treated with a great deal of respect at the present time. Both figure very prominently in the National Curriculum.

It is important to remember that for most children their introduction to some of the best books in our language will come through these two activities.

Evidence

The intuition of classroom practitioners has recently been backed by reliable research about the value of story which is worth describing in some detail.

Gordon Wells's Bristol Study involved a representative sample of 128 children. Half of this group was observed between the ages of three and a half and five plus, the other half from 15 months onwards. Half of this second group, (that is, 32 children) continued to participate in this study throughout their primary education.

This might seem to be a tiny sample on which to base substantial claims about language development. It is the longitudinal nature of the work that makes it so impressive. The 32 children were studied virtually from the time they began to talk until they were ready to enter secondary schooling. During that time teachers, parents and the children themselves were interviewed, and tests and assessments were carried out frequently. Most important of all, a large number of observations were made. It is these observations which give such strength to the investigation. Natural conversations, both at home and at school, were tape recorded at regular intervals. The participants were not aware exactly when the recorder was switched on, hence the talk which was collected was less likely to be artificial and contrived.

The major influence on the language development of these children was the home. A literate family environment was crucial and the most important factor within it was the sharing of stories. The Bristol Study backs up work done in the fifties and sixties which identified family literacy as a potent influence on educational achievement. Wells, however, goes further than either Fraser or the Manchester Survey of the Plowden Report because he has pinpointed what seems to be the essential influence – the sharing of stories.

The findings of the Bristol Survey have to be interpreted positively. If one accepts too readily that children from extremely literate families have such an advantage that their being overtaken or even caught up with is virtually impossible, then story-telling and reading in classrooms are invalidated before they even begin. More positively, we should be sharing stories for both short and long term reasons. They should

- augment what has already taken place in the home;
- compensate for its absence in some family environments;
- provide a model for families where story-telling and story-reading needs to be encouraged;
- encourage children to be interested in these activities so that their language skills and, ultimately, the skills of their children will be developed more effectively.

Story-telling skills

Two important points need to be made at the outset. First, this section concentrates more on story-telling skills than on those associated with reading stories aloud. There are several reasons for this. Story-telling has tended to become neglected. Yet it occupies an important place in the National Curriculum. In addition, many of the skills are similar for both activities. So although the main thrust is concerned with the telling of stories, story-reading skills will be dealt with in a way which avoids repetition.

The second point is that most primary schoolteachers become adept at telling and reading stories because they practise both arts. They may need to do no more than skim over much of this chapter unless they feel particularly insecure about their performance. Beginners, however, will benefit from a closer scrutiny. Some of the points which will be made might appear to be little more than commonsense but it is surprising how simple factors, overlooked in the hurly-burly of classroom life, can often influence effectiveness in a disproportionate way.

Some people are natural story-tellers: most of us need practice. Teachers in training often make the mistake of assuming that because these activities are extremely popular with children and are unlike other lessons, careful planning is not really necessary. Often they appear to be relieved that they are telling or reading a story when tutors visit them, possibly because they think that they will not be subjected to the close scrutiny which accompanies other types of lesson. Perhaps they think that they are not really teaching. Occasionally when my advice has been sought about a suitable book it has been dismaying to see it located quickly and read to a class with no preparation whatsoever. Such an approach is far too cavalier. Only the very experienced teacher might risk it from time to time as an experiment in sharing a story from scratch.

A survey of the advice available to teachers shows that most of it comes from experts associated with the library service. Three of the most distinguished contributors in this respect have been Marie Shedlock, Ruth Sawyer and Eileen Colwell. All three wrote authoritative texts on the subject which are still in use today. Eileen Colwell, the only survivor in this trio, continued to tell stories to both adults and children in her retirement until recently.

Why does the expertise seem to be confined in this way? First, storytelling is usually one of the principal ways by which librarians encourage children's interest in the library. In terms of contact they are not subject to the many demands which children make of teachers. They are therefore more likely to be able to concentrate on storytelling rather more than most teachers can. Second, their form of story-telling is free of many classroom constraints because their audience is usually a voluntary one. Books by writers associated with the library service are authoritative and full of enthusiasm. If they have a disadvantage it is that consideration of classroom conditions is rarely dealt with. When teachers do write about the subject, their texts tend to be more practical in this respect. An excellent example is *Literature and the Young Child*, written many years ago by Joan Cass but still available in many education libraries. Betty Rosen's recent book is equally useful.

It has sometimes been contended that librarians read and tell stories to children simply to interest them in literature and, to some extent, to promote library membership, whereas teachers tend to link these activities to other activities, which can make their audiences wary. There is nothing wrong with associating storytime with other parts of the curriculum but, of course, it can be overdone. To insist on related activities constantly is the death knell of story-telling.

Story-telling skills might be divided into three categories: preparatory skills, performance skills, and follow-up skills.

Preparatory skills

The importance of preparation should not be underestimated. Preparatory skills are: selecting the story; estimating the amount of time needed to tell it; editing the story; learning the story; planning the approach; deciding which, if any, audio-visual aids will be needed; and working out the positioning of both teller and audience. These are described in detail below.

Selecting the story

This is the most important skill of all. If the story is right then all the other factors will fit into place like a jigsaw. In my own experiments conducted with both teachers and students it rapidly became apparent that if the story was appropriate then even an indifferent performer could be successful. The reverse did not apply. Try as they might, even gifted story-tellers could not maintain the interest of their audiences for much more than ten minutes if the material was unsuitable. Of course when an excellent tale and a gifted performance coincide then the result is electrifying. That is what we should be aiming at and why we should be giving the craft rather more consideration.

It is important that the story-teller should like the story or, at the very least, respect it. Even the youngest children are perceptive enough to sense when this is not so. Marie Shedlock believed that the teller's love of a story was infectious.

Told stories have usually to be short because they will normally be completed on one telling. True, it is possible to serialise stories but this requires much skill and, even then, the serialisation cannot be too prolonged, especially if very young children are involved.

With young children it is only the most frightening stories which should be avoided. The presence of ghosts, for example, is a worrying factor. This does not mean that stories should be snug, safe and entirely devoid of excitement. Most comics for young children are rather like this. Yet giants, witches and the like present few fears to children. Once out of infancy most children like to be frightened anyway, just as long as they know that the event is make-believe. How many times are infants chased screaming upstairs by parents pretending to be monsters or giants only to beg for the event to happen all over again once it is terminated? And when a story is being shared with a fairly large audience, being mildly frightened is not an unpleasant experience.

Most stories will originate from books but the written word should not be exclusive. Before deciding to depend entirely upon it teachers should check if they can

- make up their own stories;
- remember any stories from their childhood which they could tell;
- trace any examples of local folk lore.

Parents and other relatives, as well as teachers, often create their own characters and weave simple stories of everyday life around them. Usually the characters are children. Their real life contemporaries find them fascinating.

Some of the stories which teachers encountered in their own childhood can be adapted for telling. They will usually be personalised and embellished by individual interpretation. There is absolutely nothing wrong with this. Indeed that is the way that most folk tales develop. Genuine folk tales, in fact, abound in every region. Some of them can be traced orally and a little research in local libraries and bookshops can assist the process. The creation of stories like these is considered in more detail in Chapter 3. Meanwhile three examples of local legends adapted by teachers for young audiences are given. It will quickly become obvious that such legends and folk tales do not have to be ancient: many of them can be obtained from grandparents.

---

1. *The Roodee*

Many centuries ago, severe drought plagued North Wales. In the absence of her Lord, the devout Lady of the Manor prayed for rain daily before a large wooden statue of the Virgin. Eventually her prayers were answered but the subsequent deluge was accompanied by a wild storm which toppled the statue, crushing the Lady to death. On his return the Lord of the Manor decreed that the statue should be tried for murder. It was sentenced to death and cast into the river Dee. The statue (which held a cross or 'rood') was washed up at Chester where it was rescued by monks. The site is not far from Chester Racecourse which is known as the Roodee (Rood-Dee?).

2. *The Spirit Pictures of Harrington School*

As he walked home one summer's afernoon in the 1920s a young boy saw what he thought was a head illuminated in a high window in his primary school. By early evening the news had spread and a large crowd gathered to witness what was now thought to be the head of Christ or the Virgin. It was not until lunchtime of the following day that a harassed headteacher provided an explanation and the crowd, not entirely convinced, dispersed.

School windows were just as prone to vandalism in the 1920s as they are today and local authorities just as cautious about expenditure. The replacement glass had originally been used in a shop window and an advertisement had been incorporated. This had not been entirely eradicated. Furthermore, the caretaker had cleaned the window with paraffin the previous day. The 'Spirit Pictures' were in fact a combination of the advertisement and the sunlight shining on the remains of the paraffin and creating a rainbow effect.

(The deputy head of this school once contributed to one of my courses. She could find no mention of the event in the official log book. But the caretaker remembered that his predecessor had heard about it from the caretaker who had actually wielded the paraffin-soaked rag. This is an excellent example of how folk tales develop.)

3. *Tasker the Tramp*

Not so many years ago, a tramp lived in a cabin made of driftwood in the sand dunes of Formby, near Liverpool. A popular local character, he was to be seen in the village each Saturday doing his shopping. Acts of kindess were repaid by gifts of shellfish and wild fruit left on doorteps. Eventually, this harmless old man became ill and was taken to hospital where he died. During his absence his cabin was set alight and razed to the ground.

People have lived in these sand dunes fairly frequently, especially during the summer months. A year or two ago a former soldier who had been sapper in the second World War made an underground home in the dunes and lived there until driven out by the cold of a particularly severe winter.

Attractive as such legends are, the main sources of material for story-tellers are the myths, legends, fairy tales and folk lore of our own and other cultures. Surprisingly, they have often been neglected in the past, probably because they have become categorised as 'fairy stories'. Most investigations of children's reading interests show that while fairy stories are popular with infants they are regarded as babyish by older pupils. Possibly junior school children who think that they are too old for such stories have rarely been introduced to the *Goose Girl* or *Bluebeard* to say nothing of the classical Greek and Roman legends. And *Beowulf* is exciting enough for even the most sophisticated eleven-year-old. A wealth of such material is available. My own favourites are listed at the end of this chapter.

Quite apart from the fact that myths, legends and folk tales offer a most useful basis for multi-cultural education, they possess a format which is the quintessence of stories told. Most of them are short and after a brief introduction an element of conflict is quickly identified. The story then progresses steadily to a climax and then rapidly subsides. Good almost invariably overcomes evil and both beginnings and endings tend to be stylised. Dialogue is frequent and repetitive phrases occur often. In other words, they have a pattern which suggests that most of them were told long before they were ever written down. They are thus the story-teller's natural material.

Other kinds of stories can, of course, also be used. One can find collections of contemporary short stories for both infants and juniors and the best of them can be selected for telling. Many books, although concerned with a central character or group, are in fact a collection of episodes some of which might be adapted for story-telling. If the writing is effective, each one will be a story in its own right. Many well known authors have written episodic material. They include Enid Blyton, Richmal Crompton, Arthur Buckeridge and Norman Hunter.

Time span

It does not take long for the novice story-teller to realise that a tale must not be too long. Even the most talented word spinner will be unable to hold a young audience for much longer than 25 minutes at a time. Twenty minutes is in fact more realistic and, for very young children, no more than 10. Exactly what comprises 20 minutes worth of story is not always easy for the beginner to estimate although the ability to do this develops quickly. If there are initial doubts, then practice readings can be timed with a stopwatch.

Editing

This is not a particularly difficult task with most of the material which is likely to be used. The oral tradition of so much of it ensures that. Here and there strange sounding names of people and places might need altering. Children like exotic words but if, for instance, too many characters have long, unfamiliar names, they might well become confused. Generally, editing should be fairly simple and economic. It is most important that the general style of a traditional tale should not be altered. It is inconceivable that 'Who's that trip-trapping over my bridge?' should be eliminated from *The Three Billy Goats Gruff*, or that 'Little Pig, Little Pig, let me come in' should suffer a similar fate.

Learning the story

Most stories which are told are not difficult to memorise. Often there are so many repetitive phrases that the actual performance can be extremely competent after just a few attempts. Parents who start out reading traditional tales to their children often begin to tell them after a while because they know them off by heart.

There is no need to be word perfect but it is surprising how well stories can be memorised with constant practice. After an initial reading the first practice attempt will probably be hesitant but usually it takes no more than one more practice run to achieve reasonable competence. Some story-tellers like to use a mirror to practise with, others use a tape recorder. Both assist in determining how the story will be presented in terms of pace, emphasis, gesture and other related story-telling skills.

Once the story is memorised it is useful to make a note of the critical points on a small piece of card. This can be held in the hand during the actual performance as an insurance against forgetting the plot. This story-teller's prompt can usually be dispensed with once the beginner gains in confidence.

Planning the approach

When will the story be told? In many schools the last part of the afternoon is reserved for the activity. There is nothing wrong with this. Quite apart from the practical aspect (there is little clearing away or tidying up to be done after a story) it is a warm, friendly, sociable ending to the school day. Many other times, however, will do just as well. Story can be used as a transition period between two sharply contrasting activities, say Physical Education and Mathematics. It tends to have a calming influence. I have seen it used intelligently on a rainy morning when two stray dogs were chasing around the hall immediately outside the classroom and a stream of children were coming and going for remedial lessons. Science was quite impossible until the situation was changed by a story-telling session.

Decisions need to be made about the relationship between the story and the rest of the curriculum. Is it a random choice which contributes in a general way to the language programme or is it, say, one of a series of legends from other lands? Has it religious or historical links? Provided there is room for flexibility, might a term's programme of story-telling be worked out rather than planning a week at a time?

Use of audio-visual aids

Many story-tellers claim that all that is needed is a good story, an effective personality and an audible voice. Although aids of one sort or another can be useful, critics are only too eager to point out that they can be a distraction. Some years ago, one of my students learned an exciting extract from 'The Iron Man' by Ted Hughes. This was accompanied by a large cardboard model with flashing electric eyes. It was an enterprising attempt but the eyes had to be disconnected fairly quickly. If this had not been done many children would have ignored the story.

It is in any case unrealistic to expect busy teachers to provide this sort of back-up for every story session. Older primary pupils would certainly become cynical if a teacher delved into a box of tricks before each story. Used carefully, however, visual aids can be helpful.

Story-tellers in libraries sometimes employ a simple ritual to commence their work. A candle is lit, a gong is sounded. Sometimes costumes are used. In classrooms the approach is usually less elaborate. Some teachers make use of music and song. Some play a guitar as an introduction or an ending to a story, others are prepared to sing if the occasion presents itself. These activities seem to be more natural than dressing up. Taped background music can also be effective although matching it to the appropriate point of a story is not always easy. Rarely will one piece sustain a story's changing moods. It is better to select just one piece for the beginning, the end or the climax. Slides of appropriate photographs can also be used although this usually involves blacking out the room. This last point emphasises the weak point of depending too much on audio-visual aids; if the machinery does not work immediately when film-slide or recorded music are being used then the momentum of a story will be lost. If success at the flick of a switch cannot be fairly certain a more simple approach should be adopted.

Pictures and models are much more commonly used. A model Spanish galleon, for instance, could be used to introduce a story about pirates. It is a good idea to reveal an illustration at the appropriate point in a story, keeping it hidden behind a blackboard or easel until it is needed. Young children also appreciate the use of a felt board to which various characters and objects are added as the story builds up. However, it must be emphasised that, above all, the story is the thing.

Location

Although the classroom is the usual setting, if a library room or a reading corner is available the conditions there might be more favourable. Comfort is essential. Young children tend to sit around the teacher's chair in a semi-circle. Their attention span is likely to be related to the hardness of the floor. Cushions and carpets help to create the right conditions.

Older pupils tend to remain at their desks. In these circumstances there is no need to request children to sit bolt upright to ensure attention. Story should be a relaxing experience and heads resting on arms or eyes staring into space do not signify lack of interest.

When pupils are desk-based the teacher might choose to stand while telling the story. The conventional position at the front of the room has one disadvantage. As the diagram indicates, eye contact cannot be maintained with everyone. To compensate for this it is a good idea to move position once or twice during a story.

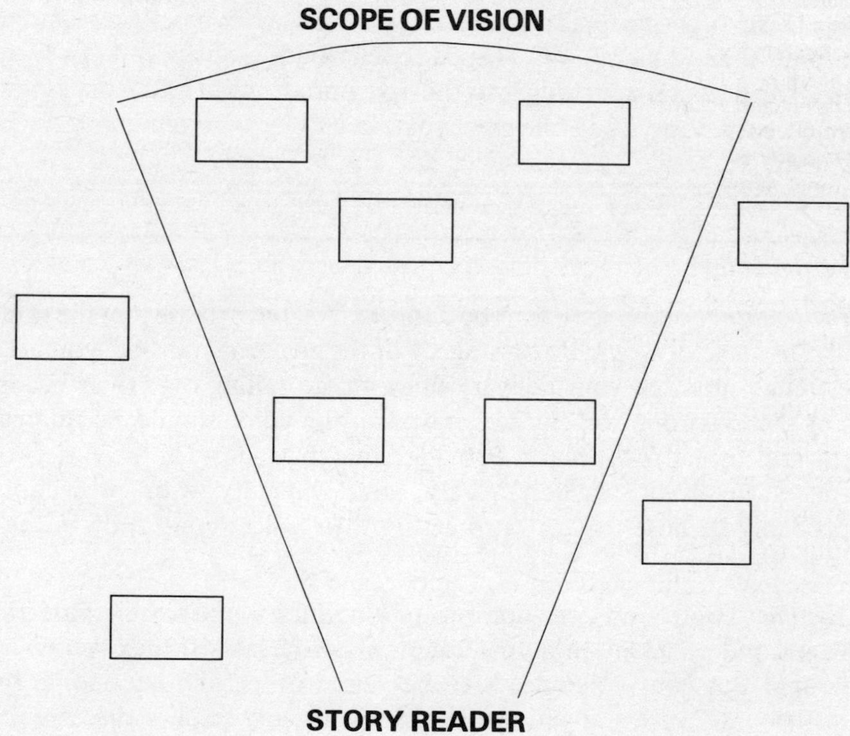

Performance skills

If the preliminary skills are taken seriously, then the performance is likely to be much more effective. Nevertheless, the way in which a story is told contributes a great deal to its success.

Performance skills fall into two main categories, verbal and non-verbal. Save for one, it is not really possible to place these skills in any hierarchical order. Eye contact is the essential skill. Without it you are really telling the story to yourself rather than to an audience. As for the other skills, individuals use them differently. One story-teller might use gesture to great effect; another might make impressive use of emphasis and the space between words. Experienced performers take most of these skills for granted although it does not harm them to re-assess their approach from time to time. The beginner should consider all of them.

Verbal skills	Intermediate skills	Non-verbal skills
Projection	Empathy	Eye contact
Volume	Enthusiasm	Pausing
Pace		Facial gesture
Tone		Body movement
Emphasis		
Inflection		
Dialogue		
Dialect and accent		
Introductions		
High points		
Conclusions		

Verbal skills

Projection: Your voice has to be audible. You have to use it in the same way as an actor would do on stage. For the group at your feet you need to make sure that your delivery does not go sailing over their heads. For the classroom or any larger space, the voice should be 'aimed' towards the half-way mark. Provided that they allow for the variety of spaces involved, teachers rarely have difficulty with projection, probably because they are projecting their voices constantly in their everyday work.

Volume: Projection does not imply that you have to shout. To do so would put off many in your audience, particularly if they were very young. But your voice needs to be raised on certain occasions, for instance to express anger, while sadness usually implies that a voice should be lowered. Whispers must obviously be stage whispers if they are to mean anything. A story inevitably generates change of volume as it changes mood. This has to be interpreted correctly. Uniform volume will create boredom and even somnolence.

Pace: If uniformity of volume is sleep inducing then uniform pace does the same job with even greater speed. Some years ago I listened to a fairly experienced student who, admittedly, was reading rather than telling a story. It was the first chapter of *The Silver Sword*. Its plot is rapid, at times headlong. Yet the reader's delivery was slow and deliberate. After ten minutes of increasing restlessness he paused to enquire if the events outside the window were so much more interesting than his story. He had not realised that it was the singer, not the song.

The shape of a story will determine the pace. When the excitement is intense or events change rapidly, your delivery will be quick; with a more gradual build up you will be much more deliberate. It is important to remember that with young children you should never talk too quickly. If you do, they might not really hear you. The measured pace of infant and nursery teachers is often ridiculed but there is no doubt that they know what they are doing.

Tone: A monotone also induces boredom. Story telling demands a variety of tones serious, light-hearted, solemn, amused depending on the situation. Discernment here should not be difficult.

Emphasis: Clearly, when telling a story we need to give some words more emphasis than others. However, this can be overdone and such efforts to make a story 'bright' and 'lively' can distract attention from the story itself. Marie Shedlock thought that emphasis was often overused and could create artificiality, particularly with small groups. She preferred a conversational rather than an emphatic approach.

Inflection: At the end of a story and, on occasions, at the end of a number of consecutive sentences, we tend to lower our voices. It is virtually imbedded in our approach to story-telling. Does this have to be consistently so? Should some stories, and some sentences, end on a high note? Certainly it would add an element of variety.

Dialogue: Most good stories contain conversation. There should not be too much, otherwise the story will become confusing. Having to append statement after statement with 'said John' 'said Jean' impedes a story's continuity. Distinguishing between two voices is not difficult if one character is young and the other is old or if they are male and female, but if there are no marked contrasts then this type of variation is best left alone. There was a 'Jackanory' programme in which Kenneth Williams told a fairy story about a five-headed dragon. He was unable to resist the temptation to use a different voice for every head but even his considerable talents proved unequal to the task.

Dialect and accent: If you are telling the ballad of the Lambton Worm to an audience from the North East of England the listeners will have no difficulty in understanding exactly what 'a muckle heed, a geet big gob and geet big goggly eyes' means. (The spoken version is rather more difficult than the written.) Tell it elsewhere and it might not be so easy. It is only worth attempting dialect if you can use it convincingly and if it will be understood. Accents pose fewer problems but the use of more than one variation in a story is inadvisable. In yet another 'Jackanory' programme William Rushden was reading an extract from Winnie the Pooh. In typical Rushden style Tigger was given an Indian accent while Roo spoke like an Australian. But this was difficult to maintain and at times Eeyore became an Australian too.

The performance skills described above are specific. Others are more general but are just as important. The introduction, climax and conclusion of a story all demand careful verbal treatment.

Introductions: Traditional tales will usually start conventionally: 'There was once . . .', There was a time . . .', 'A long time ago . . .' and, of course, 'Once upon a time . . .'. If the stories are not traditional they will need a carefully thought out introduction which states, quite simply, the setting of the story. Tales told are rarely serialised but when they are an introduction must be used on each occasion. It should not be assumed that the listeners will automatically remember what has gone before.

High points: A story does not necessarily progress steadily towards its climax. Sometimes crisis after crisis, twist after twist occur until the final solution is reached. On each occasion there should be some indication that this is a critical part of the story. The pace might increase, the voice might be raised or become more emphatic. And the climax of the tale should be the most important high point of all.

Conclusions: 'You have a tale', 'Here ends my tale' 'And they lived happily ever after', 'This is the end', 'This is my story' and similar conventional endings should normally be used with traditional tales. They represent the final sign post, showing the audience that a story has at last arrived at its destination. Young children need and appreciate these signals. They will not normally thank you for a story which is left suspended with no clear ending. Older juniors, however, appreciate the suspense of an open-ended conclusion, often volunteering to provide their own ending. 'And where they went, nobody knows' . . . is irresistible to many nine and ten-year-olds.

Non-verbal skills

Eye contact: Story-telling presents few problems for the employment of this crucial skill, largely because there is no book to distract your gaze. Eye contact should thus be fairly constant, moving gradually across an audience rather like a searchlight. Quite apart from establishing empathy and social contact this skill is a vital control factor. To quell disruption or inattention with a verbal tirade would ruin a story: a fixed gaze, rather like the Ancient Mariner's, is usually effective and much more practical.

Pausing: The space between words can be just as effective as the words themselves. The introduction of a story should be followed by a slight pause before the teller continues. There should often be a slightly longer pause before the last few phrases of a high point or story climax. In this way, a space is created in which the sense and impact of a story can become more clear. The ultimate pause is the one after a story's conclusion. As far as possible, the teller should resist the temptation to break this silence. Nine times out of ten the audience can be relied upon for that.

Facial gesture: This can be overdone. A story-teller whose facial expression changes by the second is in danger of becoming a not very competent clown. Nevertheless, a number of accepted signals and their related emotions should be considered. Everyone realises the significance of the upturned mouth, the raised eyebrows, the wrinkled brow. What is important is the way in which they unite a story-teller with an audience. Perhaps the most important gesture is a smile because it conveys the pleasure of this shared experience.

Body movement: As a nation, we are relatively undemonstrative. A flurry of hand movements would therefore bemuse most young audiences. Pointing, wagging a finger or the slight wave of a hand can all be helpful in enhancing meaning. This type of gesture is used frequently in one style of story-telling which will be examined later in this chapter. It should also be remembered that leaning towards an audience conveys security and confidence, leaning back might indicate shock or surprise at an incident in the story, and over-close proximity (that is, the invasion of a person's space) might be used to convey menace.

Intermediate skills

Lying between verbal and non-verbal skills are two extremely important factors which contribute to the overall success of story-telling. These are empathy and enthusiasm.

Empathy: This reinforces the fact that story-telling is a shared experience. As the story unfolds, the teller needs to try develop in the audience a sensitivity towards its characters and plot. Thus, the teller might complete one section with a comment, such as 'That's exciting, isn't it?; or 'What on earth is going to happen now?'; or 'I wonder what you would have done if that had happened to you?'. After a short pause for reaction the story will be recommenced. This conspiratorial approach helps to create an atmosphere of caring for and understanding of the story and its characters.

Enthusiasm: It is difficult to define exactly how this is conveyed. Yet without it most stories are lost. The story-teller has to show a keen interest in the tale, in its telling and in the audience's response. This involves both verbal and non-verbal skills, of which tone and gesture are perhaps the most important.

Follow-up skills

Librarians have an admirable approach. When a story is completed it is time to go home or to tell another one. Teachers, beset by timetables and curriculum demands, cannot always do this. Nevertheless, the urge to pounce on one's audience with a volley of questions once a story has been concluded should be resisted. How would most theatre or cinema goers react to an interrogation once the performance was over?

The end of a story should be followed by a fairly lengthy pause. In all probability it will be the children who will break the silence. If this does not happen it is often better to move on to something else. That does not necessarily imply that the story has been a failure.

From time to time story-telling will be related to other activities.

Drama, discussion, written work, art and craft can all be linked to story. A closer examination of story in the classroom occurs in Chapter 2.

Story-reading

Most writers do not create their books with the intention that they should be read aloud. A well written book is not necessarily one which can be read to children successfully. In addition, the very act of reading a book to an audience means that in most cases the reader will be holding the book, which places severe limitations on their performance skills. It is these two factors – finding the right books and reading from them – which determine most of the differences between story-telling and story-reading.

Selecting the book

Selecting the right book is a crucial preliminary skill. There is little enough time available for story-reading. It should not be wasted on triviality. Selections can be made from myths, legends, fairy tales, children's classics and good quality contemporary fiction including collections of short stories. Genre should also be varied: the all embracing 'adventure' stories, books about family life, mysteries, historical novels, fantasy, school stories and so on. There is some danger of being over ambitious. An unvaried programme of the very best books can lead to literarary indigestion. But most teachers are capable of discerning quality in children's literature and while the choice should not always be limited to the very best of books it should never sink too low. Personally, I would rarely read an Enid Blyton book to a class. Her popularity is beyond question but I think that there are so many better books which might be used.

Some of the very best books are difficult to read aloud to a young audience. For example, Richard Adams' *Watership Down* contains many accounts of what might be best described as rabbit mythology. These are only indirectly related to the rest of the book. Stevenson's magnificent *Treasure Island* has an extemely involved plot. On one occasion when I read it to top juniors one girl said to me, 'I like this book but I don't understand what is happening'.

Books with lengthy descriptions can also cause problems, yet many authors enjoy writing descriptive passages. John Steinbeck recognised that this might cause irritation to some readers and coined the expression 'Hooptedoodle' for his tendency to play with words. In one of his best-selling books he actually headed several chapters 'Hooptedoodle 1', 'Hooptedoodle 2' and so on, so that his readers might skip them if they wished to concentrate on the story. An example of Hooptedoodle in children's fiction is 'The Piper at the Gates of Dawn', an allegorical chapter in *The Wind in the Willows*. Whenever I have read the book to children I have omitted it. Yet on one occasion I was upbraided by a seven-year old who realised what I had done. You cannot please all of your audience all of the time.

It is possible to allow your own enthusiasm for a book to cloud your judgement. Despite my admiration for Henry Williamson's *Tarka the Otter* I have never been able to read it sucessfully to eleven-year olds mainly because Williamson used so much description in his work.

The implication of all of this for the story-reader is that success cannot be very certain without careful editing. With the exception of *Tarka the Otter*, all of the books mentioned above can be used after careful scrutiny. This point reinforces my own impatience with story-readers who attempt to make use of a book with little or no preparation.

Editing

The amount of time which the reading of a story will occupy needs to be estimated. Clearly, many books need to be serialised. Many of those you will be dealing with will contain as many as 40,000 words; a few like *Watership Down*, will have more than 100,000. So you need to work out:

- how much of the text can be eliminated;
- whether what remains needs to be read in its entirety.

To illustrate the need for this second consideration I will go back to my own schooldays. As a fourth year junior I enjoyed listening to Stevenson's other well known novel, *Kidnapped*. Readings took place during the last half hour of every Thursday afternoon. No doubt my teacher had done some editing but it took almost the entire school year to complete this book. Even where storytime is increased from once a week there will never be sufficient hours in the day to read even a tiny fraction of the books available. After stricter editing, more books might be read from start to finish: others might be started then abandoned: yet others might be commenced at the half-way stage. The point of story-reading is not solely to complete books: it is just as important to introduce a wide variety of interesting material.

Editing also requires that the following points should be considered:

- Does the plot move fairly quickly?
- Are the main characters convincing?
- How descriptive is the writing?
- Is the amount of conversation sufficient, yet not in such quantity as to cause the listener confusion?

By bearing these point in mind, you can eliminate excessive descriptive writing as well as complicated conversations which could cause listeners to be uncertain about which character is actually talking. If the plot slows or becomes too complicated then decide whether it is possible to proceed from one high point to another with the help of short but clear descriptions of what happens in between. By making use of this type of ruthless editing you will be able to use some books which could not be read aloud in their entirety.

In most books there will be some words which will not be easily understood, even allowing for contextual clues. Pausing during a reading session to explain them is unwise. They might be substituted by more simple words or, preferably, be written on the blackboard beforehand with their meanings explained. There should not be too many of these words. When such a situation occurs, the book is obviously not suitable for reading aloud.

Serialisation is another important factor to bear in mind when editing. To end a session with the conclusion of a chapter may not be good enough. Chapters are used by authors for a variety of reasons and their endings are not always memorable. Nor is it sensible to allow the ending to be dictated by the school bell, picking up where one left off next time. The best approach is the 'powder keg' method. No doubt readers will recall the serialised films they watched in their youth where, for example, the heroine might be tied to the railway line just as a train steamed over the horizon. It was obvious that she would be rescued but that would happen on the following Saturday. Regular watchers had no difficulty in remembering the events of the previous week. Soap operas make use of the same technique. It is not difficult to find suitable points of suspense in a book. The effects of making use of them can often be striking. Usually, there are verbal protests, usually good humoured, when the conclusion of a reading session ends like this. It certainly leaves an audience asking for more and there will be few children who do not recall what has happened so far when the book is picked up on the next occasion.

Reading from a book makes the use of audio-visual aids more difficult. Usually they are confined to pictures and models. With young children pictures in the actual book being read are almost invariably used in this way. They are usually large and attractive and the children, normally at the teacher's feet, are close enough to see them clearly. Infant teachers develop a technique which could be described as 'reading sideways'; that is, they hold the book to one side of them with the print and pictures facing the audience. They can read in this way not only because the print is large but also because the texts are short and fairly easily learned after one or two readings. The very large books which are now available are particularly useful in this respect.

For beginners the reading position will usually be static. The elementary skills of holding a book, reading from it and trying to maintain eye contact take some time to master. I recall the very first occasion I was observed as a student teacher. I was reading a lengthy poem which gave me ample time to demonstrate what skills I had. The tutor's written comments were complimentary save for a sting in the tail. His final sentence was: 'You should surely have noticed that numerous boys were changing into football boots at the back of the classroom.' In fact, I was not able to. Holding a book and reading from it was as much as I could manage: I could not maintain sufficient eye contact.

Ideally, the book should be placed on a flat, preferably sloping, surface. This dispenses with the necessity to hold it. One of my colleagues carries a small, portable lectern around with him for story-reading sessions. Although most beginners rapidly improve, eye contact always requires a much more concentrated effort when reading, as opposed to telling, stories. This makes movement around the classroom quite difficult. Most readers sit rather than stand. Today it is much more common for teachers to place their chairs in front of the desk or at the side rather than create a barrier by sitting behind it. Some actually sit on it.

In terms of performance skills, non-verbal factors, other than eye control, are relatively unimportant, mainly because it is extremely difficult to make use of them. To compensate for this, verbal skills have to be accentuated. Pace, tone and emphasis should assume much greater importance than in story-telling and introductions have to be carefully prepared. One should give a brief summary of the book and its setting without revealing too much. Occasionally this can be very difficult. For example, if introducing Gene Kemp's book *The Turbulent Term of Tike Tiler* the reader would have to avoid mentioning that Tike was a girl, otherwise much of the book's enjoyment would be spoiled.

Both empathy and enthusiasm will tend to centre around the book rather than the reading of it. Knowledge and understanding of a book, which implies that it has been read frequently, impresses young audiences.

Finally, story-reading presents one problem rarely encountered in story-telling. Books which are serialised are sometimes rejected by some of the listeners. There is little need to seek the audience's advice in this respect: individuals' reactions can usually be clearly seen on their faces.

What should one do if story-reading is not going well? It would be a mistake to abandon a book after one reading session. Some books, even after careful editing, start slowly. But if after three readings a book is still creating a largely negative impact, then it is best to give it up. No great harm will have been done. Indeed, some individuals might want to read the book for themselves. It is much better to adopt this approach than to plough on regardless.

Style in reading and telling stories

At some time or another skilful tellers and readers of tales will take stock of their talents, adjust or alter them and, in most cases, become more efficient. Depending on how these skills are put together, certain styles of telling and reading stories will emerge. There are a number of clearly identifiable styles. These are:

- undemonstrative;
- dramatic;
- collaborative;
- ritualistic;
- unseen;
- remote.

The first three of these are the styles most likely to be adopted by classroom practitioners. Inevitably, there will be some overlap. For example, someone who adopts a basically undemonstrative approach might also use a limited number of dramatic and collaborative techniques.

The undemonstrative style

Tellers and readers associated with the library service are usually strong advocates of this style. It is the story which counts. Audio-visual aids, dramatic gestures and movements are regarded as superfluous. The location is austere, probably in order to focus attention on the performer. Even the use of verbal skills is not overdone. Emphasis is on the quality of the story, the performer's enjoyment of it and the quietness of the delivery.

The dramatic style

Here, the tendency is to act out the story. The teller (and it is much more likely to be a teller than a reader) moves around, gesticulating, shouting, even stamping. The performance is lively and, usually, good fun. Children can accept this style in small doses. If it is overdone, the relevant skills are neglected in favour of acting. Eileen Colwell tells of a fond parent who used *Goldilocks and the Three Bears* as a vehicle for charging about, using a variety of voices and generally being amusing. When his version of the tale had been completed he was met with the comment: 'But when are you going to tell me the story of Goldilocks and the Three Bears?' Clearly, the story had become lost amid a welter of drama. A variation of this style is often used when puppets are used for story-telling purposes.

The collaborative style

In order to retain attention, story-tellers in times past frequently employed audience participation. They made use of choruses, of repetition of several sentences with only one or two words changing from one occasion to the next, and they even assigned parts of the story to individual listeners. Today it is a technique beloved by pantomine performers. Teachers on the whole do not employ this style enough despite the fact that many stories and books can be adapted to accommodate it. Variations include cumulative poems (for instance, 'The House that Jack Built'), and the use of puppets and stories or poems which include what is usually described as finger play (that is counting and acting out movements using the hands).

An impressive exponent of the collaborative style was H. E. Todd, author of the 'Bobby Brewster' series of books. In his retirement he delighted children in many parts of the world by inviting them to participate actively in his stories. For instance, an amusing phrase would be repeated at intervals until the children joined in.

The ritualistic style

This is story-telling formalised. The story is introduced in a set way. For example, candles might be lit. Some sort of costume is often worn.

This style is often seen at folklore festivals and librarians sometimes make use of it too. A modified version can be used in schools. Young story-tellers, in particular, will enjoy dressing up for the part.

The unseen voice

Taped stories are becoming an increasingly important part of storytime in schools. Whether or not teachers wish to create their own taped stories or simply rely on cassettes and radio broadcasts, it is useful to have some understanding of this style. The unseen reader depends almost entirely on verbal skills. That is why so many actors are used for cassette recordings. Thus the emphasis is on tone, volume, pace, the use of dialogue, accents, dialect and the space between words. Overdone, this style can verge on the ridiculous. But, at its best, it is an extremely effective form of story-telling which can be used with audiences of varying size. The nostalgia of many adults for 'Children's Hour' and 'Listen with Mother' should vouch for that.

The remote voice

Story telling can be filmed. It is, perhaps, the least natural style of all but one which is becoming quite common.

Story-tellers and readers on film have a number of advantages. They are often talented actors, have much more time for rehearsal and have far more facilities available to them than teachers will ever have. Their great disadvantage is that they are neither fish nor fowl. They lack the verbal magnetism of the unseen reader and, despite their visibility, their contact with their audience is tenuous. This is well worth thinking about. Comedians performing on television usually need the reassurance of a live audience. By contrast, the story-teller or reader on TV or film has no idea how the very large but unseen audience is reacting. It is a style which needs a great deal of support from audio-visual material. Probably the most successful of these programmes has been 'Jackanory' and it is interesting to note the methods by which its producers strived to retain children's interest. The length of the programme was sensible. Fifteen minutes is just about right. To counteract the weakest feature of this style – watching an image reading a story – a large number of pictures and drawings were used, sometimes at the rate of two per minute. Often the reader was given an attractive scenic background which was sometimes changed during the programme. The reader was not always static; occasionally there would be a movement from one spot to another. Such arrangements were essential to the success of the programme. Without them it would have been difficult to attract a large audience.

Much of this might not seem to be particularly relevant to the world of the classroom. It seems quite likely, however, that teachers and children will be involved in creating this type of story in the future; in which case, a study of this particular style is important. 'Jackanory' episodes might be videotaped to assist this process.

Summary

Most primary teachers instinctively recognise story-telling and story-reading to be important tools of their trade. Their intuition is backed up by reliable educational research.

The age-old craft of story-telling is used more frequently with young children whereas story-reading is more common in junior departments. With the introduction of the National Curriculum it is likely that this situation will change and that both crafts will be in use throughout the primary school.

Both story-telling and story reading require practice. It is possible to identify both preparatory and performance skills. These are not dissimilar for both crafts, save in emphasis. A knowledge of these skills and the willingness to practise them is likely to make both activities more effective.

The use of story figures large in the National Curriculum. How it might be used in primary school classrooms will be considered in the following chapter.

References

Bettleheim, B. (1976) *The Uses of Enchantment – The Meaning and Importance of Fairy Tales*. Thames and Hudson.

CACE (1967) *Children and their Primary Schools* (The Plowden Report), HMSO.

Cass, J. (1967) *Literature and the Young Child*. Longman.
Colwell, E. (1981) *Storytelling*. Bodley Head.
Cook, E. (1969) *The Ordinary and the Fabulous*. Cambridge University Press.
Egan, K. (1988) *Teaching as Storytelling*. Routledge.
Fraser, E. (1953) *Home Environment and the School*. University of London Press.
Pellowski, A. (1977) *The World of Storytelling*. Bowker.
Rosen, B. (1988) *And None of it was Nonsense – the Power of Storytelling in School*. Mary Glasgow Publications.
Sawyer, R. (1966) *The Way of the Storyteller*. Bodley Head.
Shedlock, M. L. (1951) *The Art of the Storyteller*. Dover.
Wells, G. (1986) *The Meaning Makers*. Hodder and Stoughton.

Other useful reading

Baker, A. and Greene, E. (1977) *Storytelling: Art and Technique*. Bowker.
Bauer, C. T. (1977) *A Handbook for Storytellers*. American Library Association.
Chambers, A. (1973) *Introducing Books to Children*. Heinemann.
Fenwick, G. and Evans, G. (1978) 'The Analysis of Story Reading Skills', *UKRA Reading*, July.
Marshall, M. (1979) *Storytelling – Practical Guides*. Youth Libraries Group.
Mears, J. and Parker, A. (1975) *Read Aloud*. Youth Libraries Group.
Moss, E. (1977) 'Storytelling', *Education 3–13*, Vol. 5, No. 1.
Todd, H. E. (1973) 'Storytelling', *Children's Literature in Education*, Sept. No. 12.
Wagner, J. A. (1975) *Children's Literature through Storytelling*. Hamilton.
Ziskind, S. (1976) *Telling Stories to Children*. H. W. Wilson and Co.

Local legends

'The Roodee' was researched by Marion Jones.
'The Spirit Pictures of Harrington School' was researched by Kath Toms.
'Tasker the Tramp' was researched by Frank Maguire.

CHAPTER 2

Story in the Classroom

In the ideal primary school teachers will be constantly telling and reading good stories by the best possible means, at the same time refining and improving their skills. That is what we should all be aiming for. It is important, however, that teachers share stories not only with children but with parents and colleagues too.

Widening the scope of the story activity

By working with more than one class, teachers can work out a story programme which enables them to gain wider experience, thereby improving their versatility. They might also increase the audience on occasions by combining their class with others. There is nothing to stop several teachers sharing a story. Alternatively, they can present different ones within the one session. Obviously, care has to be taken if there is a wide age range in the audience. While this will challenge teachers' skills, the range should not be too wide. It is not easy to find a story which interests both reception class children and top juniors.

Should the story programme be carefully worked out, whatever the approach? Long term planning on a co-operative basis will help teachers not only with story skills but with knowledge of appropriate books.

Even when applying the criteria mentioned in the preceding chapter, beginners are often at a loss when trying to work out what they can read to their class. They should not hesitate to consult their more experienced colleagues and also the local children's librarian. Slowly but surely it will be possible to build up a list of books which have been successfully presented to various classes. Even with experienced teachers there is a temptation to stick to what is already known; if this is taken too far, then the story programme will be in danger of ossifying. In any case, what went well with one class does not necessarily suit another. Story-telling and story-reading lists should be adjusted from year to year.

There is always the temptation for anyone who is reasonably knowledgeable about children's literature to produce booklists. This book endeavours to avoid this because it is my opinion that there are far too many lists, and that this creates confusion. A short starter list is provided at the end of this chapter for those who think that they need such help. I have enjoyed reading these books to children but, of course, they represent my personal choice and there is no cast-iron guarantee that what works for me will necessarily work for someone else. By far the best way to discover what to read is to compile your own list with the help of colleagues. If further advice is needed, then there is an excellent list in the Treasury of Read Alouds section of *The Read–Aloud Handbook* by Jim Trelease.

The experienced teacher will have already built up most of the skills mentioned in the previous chapter. They will have been adapted to suit the individual's talents and personality as well as the context in which the activity is taking place. Although it requires some courage, making a story-telling video-tape can often prove useful as a means of enhancing one's skills yet further. This does not work for everyone. Successful attempts can be incorporated into the story-telling programme: disasters can be dispensed with. Either way, something will have been learned.

There is yet another way by which teachers might extend their expertise. Story-telling in the community has grown in strength in recent years and it is now possible to bring skilled practitioners into schools. This should prove to be as helpful for teachers as for pupils. Details of the National Community Folktale Centre's list of story-tellers are available in the bibliography at the end of this chapter.

If we accept Gordon Wells's evidence concerning the power of story then we have to accept that its beginnings should be in the home. Teachers can play a vital part in promoting and enhancing this activity. Thus, meetings of story-tellers and readers should include parents, and schools should constantly be advising both their actual and potential customers about the value of story in the home. Much of this advice should be practical.

Story-telling groups are well developed in both USA and Canada. Skilled practitioners work alongside teachers, librarians and parents, introducing good stories, finding new ones and working out the various ways in which they can be presented. The city of Toronto, for instance, has its own storytellers guild.

Finally, an excellent way of putting this together is the Story Festival. Annual celebrations of story might be held in school departments, in whole schools or even with several schools participating. If this sounds like pie in the sky then *Storytelling: Art and Technique* by Augusta Baker and Ellen Greene is worth consulting. Story festivals are by no means uncommon in America.

The following suggestions might be helpful to teachers who would like to organise their own festival:

(1) Arrange an initial reading by a well known author or poet involving popular, well recognised work or even writing in progress.
(2) Show a videotape of a parent or teacher telling an original or well known story.
(3) Arrange a story fair in the hall and surrounding classrooms where children and adults can tell and read stories to small audiences. Costumes and visual aids should be welcomed.
(4) Show a popular film version of a story (*The Snowman*, for example).
(5) Organise story making sessions in small groups; techniques and content to be considered.
(6) Arrange a cassette carnival: small groups to select relatively short cassettes for listening to.
(7) Arrange a 'make-up-your-own-ending' contest: the audience listen to a tape produced by a parent or teacher which is terminated before the ending is obvious. Small groups work out their own conclusions.
(8) Show videos of several stories devised by groups of children.
(9) Organise a short puppet show competition.
(10) Get together story collections: creepy stories, heroic stories, family stories, etc. Pupils select one of the collections to talk about in groups of no more than 20.
(11) Encourage cumulative poems, along the lines of 'The First Day of Christmas'. Let Christmas last for 30 days and see what results.
(12) As a grand climax, a parent or teacher or writer tells a collaborative story with a great deal of audience participation, particularly towards the end.

Children as story-tellers

Children's creation of stories has, until recently, been much more encouraged in written rather than spoken form. Some of the finest exponents of story-telling have not been particularly optimistic in this respect. Marie Shedlock expressed marked doubts about the wisdom of asking children to tell stories and, years later, Eileen Colwell seemed to think that it was something which should not happen too often. Behind such doubts, perhaps, are reservations about children's ability to make use of the required skills and fears that their efforts might trivialise the craft. Yet the evidence from Story Festivals clearly implies that children can and should be involved. Furthermore, Gordon Wells's study indicated that young children make use of story narrative very frequently, a point picked in the 1970s by Harold and Connie Rosen. And the National Curriculum recognises its usefulness.

Can children tell stories in a formal, structured way? Below is an example of a five-year old's attempt to re-tell *Goldilocks and the Three Bears*:

Once upon a time there was three bears . . . there was three bears . . . three bears. There was a daddy bear, mummy bear and a baby bear. Mummy Bear made some porridge. They tasted some but it was too hot . . . so they went out . . . and then Goldilocks came. She went in the door and then she saw the three bowls of porridge. She tasted the biggest bowl. That was too hot. She tasted the middle-sized one. That was too sweet. Then she tasted the little one. It tasted just right. Then Goldilocks felt sleepy. She went to look for a chair . . . chair. First she went on the biggest chair. That was too hard. Then she went on the middle-sized chair. That was too soft. Then she went on the littlest chair. It was just right. In five minutes it broke. So she went upstairs to try the beds. First she went on the biggest bed. That was too hard. Then she went on the middle-sized bed. That was too soft. Then she went to try the littlest bed. That was just right. In one second she was already asleep. Then the three bears came . . . came . . . came and they went into the house. Daddy Bear said, 'Who's been eating my porridge?'. Mummy Bear said, Who's been eating my porridge?' 'Who's been eating my porridge?' said Baby Bear, 'and they've ate it all up.' Then they went into the dining room and they saw. Daddy Bear said, 'Who's been sitting in my chair?' 'Who's been sitting in my chair?' said Mummy Bear, 'And who's been sitting in my chair?' said Baby Bear, 'and they've broke it.' They went upstairs. They went in the bedroom. Daddy Bear said, 'Who's been sleeping in my bed?' Mummy Bear said, 'Who's been sleeping in my bed?' Baby Bear said, 'Who's been sleeping in my bed and they're still in it.' Then they went up to her . . . Goldilocks . . . then Baby Bear stole his teddy and Goldilocks was awake. She ran down the steps out of the door. She ran all the way home.

Unfortunately, a transcript cannot communicate the story-telling mode which even quite young children adopt. Nor can it fully convey the drama of the performance. Once the transcript is examined more closely it should be evident that this child has a competent control of language structure. There are only a few errors of tense and little hesitation. There is a flash of originality: note how he introduces the (his?) teddy towards the end of the transcript. It is by no means easy to do this within the tight format of a traditional tale. More important, Robert has a firm grasp of story telling techniques.

- There is a formal beginning.
- The characters are quickly established.
- The plot progresses logically.
- The necessary repetition is accurate.
- There is a formal ending.

Robert does not always find storytelling as easy as this. Without the traditional format he flounders, especially when he is unsure of a story's meaning.

... We watched a video ... Captain Cutlass ... not Captain Cutlass ... Cutlass goes to Liverpool and there were army men and there was a robot in it and there was a spaceship ... and the robot was collected to it. That's what he was looking for and he 'sploded everything but not that person ... Captain Cutlass.

Few of us will be familiar with this story but it is evident that neither the characters nor the plot have really been made clear. Also, it is much harder to retell a story seen on video than one which has been heard many times.

Even younger children can retell traditional stories with some fluency. At four years, another child tackled *The Three Little Pigs* without much difficulty. There are more individual variations. For example,

'The fourth lickle pig ...'
'So he got up at 40 o'clock ...'
'So he thinked a plan ...'
'... he set a boiling fire and a boiling pan of boiling water and the wolf came down the chimley and fell into it and the lickle pig put the lid on it and the wolf was boiled alive and he took the lickle pigs out first ...'

Even with the constraints of a traditional story, there is room for improvisation. When young children do not know the exact word required they will guess with some accuracy. And there will always be individual interpretations. It seems, for instance, that the pigs who were caught by the wolf were boiled in the same pot in which the wolf eventually met his fate. Obligingly, the teller lets them out before the wolf is finally boiled to death.

One suspects that these two young storytellers have enjoyed

listening to many stories. Not all children are so fortunate. Yet it is possible to improve a child's performance. In the next two transcripts, Paul aged 7 makes two attempts to retell a story which originated from his reading book at school.

Once upon a time the children decided that they were going to the beach. They had a picnic. Thunder and the children raced to the sea. Graham said, 'The water is lovely.' Thunder is a dinosaur. The life guard thought that Thunder was a monster. The children said, 'No, he is our friend.' The children went home.

The basic story format is evident in this transcript but listeners and readers have to make educated guesses to make a story out of it. It is, in fact, a summary of a story. Compare it with the second attempt.

One sunny day some children thought they would go to the beach and have a picnic and a splash by the sea. They have a friend called Thunder. Thunder is not a boy or a girl, he is a dinosaur, a big, green dinosaur. He is friendly and doesn't eat people. Thunder said, 'Can I come too?' 'Yes,' said the children. They had a picnic on some sand. They had food their Mum gave them. They had pop and strawberries and chocolate biscuits. Thunder had some too 'cos there wasn't any dinosaur food. When they had none left they ran to the sea. The water was lovely and blue. They splashed each other and swam about. One little boy said, 'This is like being on holiday.' There was a life guard. He was scared. 'There's a monster,' he shouted. 'Go away, monster.' The children laughed. No, he's not a monster, he is Thunder, our friend.' Thunder smiled too, he thought the life guard was silly. The children swam about more and then they went home for their tea. The end.

Here there is far more detail and the sequence of events is much more clear. There is dialogue and a certain amount of humour. This is a genuine story. What happened in the time between these two attempts? Little more than a discussion between an adult and a child about the quality of the first transcript and some suggestions as to how it might be improved.

Story-telling investigations involving children are becoming more frequent. Probably the best known was carried out by Barrie Wade. Wade wished to check whether the ability to tell stories depended upon maturation or whether the process could be accelerated by practice. In addition, he wanted to find out if parental interest was an important factor. In a well organised experiment he studied groups of five-year olds in ten schools for a period of two terms. Children who had stories read frequently to them at home and who were encouraged to tell stories quickly became more proficient than other groups who did not make use of these facilities. This might seem fairly obvious despite the fact that Wade was, in a limited way, disproving the idea that children would only develop these skills when they were ready to do so. More important, when tested eighteen months later the experimental group still maintained their advantage. Story-telling might be compared to riding a bicycle: once you have learned how to, you never forget.

Henrietta Dombey's work, though much more limited, provides further useful evidence. Tape recordings of a year's story-telling shared between a mother and her three-year old child revealed an increasing number of contributions by the child. Story was literally being shared. In a similar way, children in a nursery class were studied for a year and they also showed an increase in contributions as well as gains in confidence. Their re-told stories increased in both amount and complexity.

Dombey's associate, Caroline Fox, collected data from story-telling activities carried out with five children aged between three and a half and five and their parents. Recordings of the children re-telling stories revealed the influence of books which had been read to them in terms of structure and composition.

More recently, Phil Sandell reported on a programme conducted throughout a primary school, involving children, teachers, students and a tutor. His initial comments on his young daughter's sudden attempt to contribute to a story which he was telling her backs up the evidence provided by Henrietta Dombey. Young children in his project designed puppets and told stories about them to small audiences. The audience factor was an important one. If children can tell stories then someone should be listening. Older infants were helped to progress from merely listening to stories and making limited contributions to telling their own stories. Co-operative work included taped stories by small groups of children who edited their material until they thought that it was suitable.

Working with me for her Advanced Diploma in Children's Literature, Kath Ahern attempted a controlled experiment with a small group of seven-year olds. It would be fair to say that the environment in which these children lived was a bleak one. It was unlikely that story figured very large in their family life. Yet after only seven weeks of practice there were signs of striking improvement not unlike that in Paul's transcripts which we have already examined. This group evinced much enthusiasm for the work, showing in one way, at least, that deprivation is relative. Although there did not seem to be many books at home there was no shortage of tape recorders for them to practise their skills with.

When work like this is carried out with young children, the task in the junior department is much easier. If they are already competent the older primary pupils have scope for experiment and improvisation.

But what happens when junior pupils without much experience are asked to practise these skills? Might it be that they think such activities are babyish and beneath them? It seems not. Also working with me for a Diploma award, Rita Bibby conducted an investigation with nine year olds in an urban school. Within the space of two months four of the six children had made marked progress. One might have expected this of three of the improvers because their reading ages were high. In fact, it did appear as if some of this work did not really challenge them because it was not quite at the right level. Nevertheless, their powers of retention were at times impressive and this was obviously widening their vocabulary. Compare the original wording of part of a story with Keith's improvisation.

My beauteous one, my beauteous one,
My croco-croco dear,
By land or sea where 'er it be,
You have no single peer

Oh beauteous one, oh beauteous one,
Oh croco-croco dear,
I've never been happier
Than to be with you here.

It was not only the superior readers who improved. The pupil with the poorest reading age (one and a half years less than his chronological age) improved so much that at least two of his story-telling attempts are well worth examining. Here is an extract from his first attempt at re-telling a story.

Once there lived little dog Turpie . . . with an old woman . . . an . . . an old man. The . . . Hobyards switched on . . . they went, came through the grass and went weef, woof. They went emm, hang on, they went . . . through the house and one said, 'Break down . . . the break . . . break down the house . . . '

The transcript is, in fact, quite lengthy and even this extract gave some indication of originality. But is is hesitant and confused. Compare it to one which was recorded six weeks later.

Once there lived a crocodile. He lived on a sandbank. He was a wise old guy. Yes, he had an adorable wife and he loved her very much. He a . . . writ a poem about her la la la and la la la like that. That was it . . .

This extract from a transcript even longer than the first clearly shows increased confidence, far more ability to retain the details of a story and clever improvisation. Note how although he has forgotten the words of the poem he is prepared to demonstrate what it sounded like.

What the extract above does not show is this boy's originality, his dramatisation, his use of sound effects and his sense of humour.

Moreover, he is showing a linguistic competence far superior to anything contained in what he is able to read or write. This should give him more confidence and with luck and good guidance his talent might be transferred to other areas of the language curriculum.

How children's story-telling can be improved

Here, two questions need to be answered. What advice should we give our pupils? And, having given it, what experiences should we provide for them?

It would be futile to introduce primary school children to the variety of skills described in the previous chapter. To do so would simply overwhelm them. But they do need a framework. Four factors have already been mentioned which emerge from examination of the transcripts in this chapter. More accurately described, they are

- A formal or obvious beginning.
- Identification of main characters.
- A logical succession of events.
- A formal or obvious ending.

To these I would add:

- Use of the past tense.
- Use of the third person.
- Rhythm and fluency.

It is likely that many children will make use of these factors without thinking too much about them because if they have listened to stories the chances are that they will have assimilated the accepted mode of story-telling. The skill which develops most with practice seems to be rhythm. Listening to tapes one can sense that as a child gains in confidence so the rhythm of the story improves, and hesitancy and staccato delivery are reduced.

Two other factors should be considered. They are:

- memorisation and;
- visualisation.

Many children find it difficult to memorise stories. Perhaps we have moved too far away from rote learning in most school subjects. Yet it is surprising what a difference practice can make. It is probably best to split a story up to begin with and build it up, piece by piece. Children, like adults, will probably benefit from having a small card with the main facts of the story written on it to jog their memory.

Visualisation is a skill which some children unwittingly use when they really believe in a story. Chapter 1 mentioned the ability of skilled adult story tellers to project their enthusiasm for their stories. Some go further than this; they attempt to see the characters and their background as the tale unfolds. Gesture often helps this along but I think that it is the face and eyes in particular which convey this skill.

Ask children what they see when they tell stories. You are likely to receive some interesting answers. The chances are that many of them have been doing this without being aware of it.

What activities help children with their stories? Some of these have already been mentioned in the discussion of Story Festival material earlier in this chapter. Certainly, co-operative stories are useful. A small group might combine to plan and share the telling. They might edit the story, think of a better ending or provide some artifacts which will create additional interest. Another approach is to make use of puppets. This can help shy children who find the gaze of an audience uncomfortable. It is also likely to develop drama and dialogue effectively.

Although it can be time consuming, and should therefore be used sparingly, video-taped performance provides useful feedback to both pupils and teachers. Scrutiny of work like this assists in the analysis of story-telling skills. Barrie Wade has identified a number of these, in particular

- setting;
- episode structure;
- shape of content;
- logical order;
- centring;
- chaining.

The first four skills should be self explanatory. We have already discussed the structure of folk tales. Centring, an unfamiliar term, is the identification of subjects or actions which are important to the story. Chaining is concerned with the sequence of events. Combine the two and you are more likely to have a narrative which is clear and story-like.

Although I find some overlap in these categories, I can appreciate their usefulness to teachers who wish to improve their pupils' skills. The technical terms need not necessarily be used but children should be encouraged to see story-telling as a logical process which has an ordered framework. It might well be that these skills can be conveyed implicitly by means of excellent stories well told. But from time to time, it will do no harm to discuss how the background of a story might be introduced or how a tale might move from one event to the next.

So far, discussion has concentrated on re-telling stories. Several of the studies mentioned contain details of attempts at original work. Unfortunately, the evidence to date is not particularly convincing. This is mainly because of a number of difficulties associated with primary children making up their own stories. Often they interpret 'their own story' with one not prescribed by the teacher. Thus their telling and re-tellings are not markedly different. In any case, it is extremely difficult to determine exactly how original a story is. One has only to examine adult writing to appreciate this. How many novels with a futuristic slant owe something to the works of George Orwell or Aldous Huxley? In a similar way many children's stories are an amalgamation of several stories along with the teller's own contribution. This is evident in the transcripts which we have examined in this chapter. Personally, I do not think that the distinction between telling and re-telling stories is particularly important. More useful is the way in which the individual interprets and presents a story.

When it comes to the preparation of a story I feel uneasy about preliminary and copious written work. I prefer to think that the reverse process is more useful. That is, by constantly practising story-telling, primary children might become so familiar with story form that it is reflected in their written work.

Children as story-readers

Reading stories aloud is more difficult than story-telling because it depends so much on reading ability. These days reading aloud tends to be seen as part of the process of learning to read and, as such, has been the subject of some criticism in recent years. As a result it is a far more structured process than it used to be. At one time, reading aloud was a frequent, if not popular occurrence. In the sixties and early seventies sets of books were much more in evidence than they are today. A story would be read with individuals following it in their own copies. The trouble began when this activity was converted to reading around the class. Pupils with reading difficulties were either ignored or humiliated and extremely competent readers were often bored and irritated by the uneven pace of the various readings. This is not an approach which is seen very often these days but it has left its mark on reading aloud.

Does this mean that children should not be encouraged to read aloud? I believe not, but the activity must be treated with sensitivity and has to be carefully thought out. Children might share stories in this way in small groups. Young children often do this when they read the 'Big' books so much in vogue today. These books, often as much as a metre in length and almost as broad, have large print and attractive pictures that combine with stories which make frequent use of rhyming and repetition. It is not long before even children with acute reading difficulties are joining in the choruses.

Reading aloud stories such as these helps children to know the stories off by heart. This, of course, is a form of reading which depends to some extent upon visual memory. My son became aware of this, many years ago at the age of three. He had become fascinated with one of the Dr. Seuss books and knew it word for word. On one occasion he was asked to demonstrate his new found skill. So he 'read' the book as he sat in his bedroom and both book and audience remained downstairs.

Another useful approach is for older primary pupils to read stories to younger ones. This can be done with both groups and individuals. If the difference in age range is marked, the reader is less likely to have any difficulty with the reading material being used.

Careful selection can eliminate most difficulties. Any embarrassment about reading simple material can usually be overcome by concentrating on performance skills, particularly the dramatic effect. We have discussed these skills already. The most important ones for children are probably emphasis and pace; in non verbal terms, the pause can be used to great effect.

Schools might encourage reading aloud at all ages by organising their own programme over a public address system. By the time they leave their primary schools the great majority of pupils should have contributed to this form of story reading.

Reading aloud as part of learning to read has sometimes created the impression that the main purpose of the skill was the identification of syllables and words. Hence the lack of fluency and 'barking at print' which affects some children's early reading. If the purpose of reading aloud is linked more with reading for meaning then it is likely to become more popular. Children are more likely to read effectively when they make use of stories which they really like. Reading aloud should be done when it is fun!

Story and school subjects

Subjects in the early years understandably lack clear cut definition. Thus, for the teachers of very young children story is part of a seamless robe: it can be used to suit a variety of occasions with little artificiality. Reading, writing, number work, movement, visual and tactile experiences can all be related to story.

As children move into the junior department, however, specific subjects are given more emphasis and at first glance some of them lend themselves more readily to story than do others. Yet the persuasive and compelling nature of story can help children to make connections between what might often appear to be nothing more than disparate facts. For this to happen it is necessary to examine the possible interaction between stories and specifically defined subjects.

Integrating story is by no means new. I was attracted to many post-Plowden classrooms in the late sixties because of the magnificent friezes, models and paintings created around stories like *Treasure Island* or *Black Beauty*. An American writer, Katherine Cather, advocated this approach as early as 1919. Her ideas fitted in more comfortably with some subjects than with others. Mathematics and Science, apart from some reference to Nature Study, were ignored. And many of the ideas reflected the didactic approaches of the time. She considered, for instance, story-telling as a part of the teaching of ethics in a way which now appears rather oppressive.

Another American, Dewey Chambers, also attempted to integrate story with school subjects. In doing so, his main purpose was to avoid an over-dependence on textbooks. Chambers examined links with both the Arts and the Sciences but tended to use reference and information books rather than literature.

The work of these two experts indicates that there has been uncertainty about the ways by which integration of story into the curriculum can be achieved. History and Religious Education are subjects in which a narrative form of teaching is not uncommon. Stories centred on these subjects abound. Geography is perhaps less well endowed: nevertheless stories about discoverers and particular places can be found without too much difficulty. So can regional folklore. But what about other subject areas. For example, Mathematics, Science, Physical Education, Dance and Drama, Music, Art, Craft and Design?

Stories about inventors are not uncommon although the emphasis tends to be on science rather than maths. Science fiction is a literary genre and has been popular with older juniors for many years. Books about sports and sportspersons are fairly common; those about dancers, actors and musicians perhaps less so although they are by no means rare; nor are books about crafts and craft persons.

It would be artificial to constantly link literature with subjects in this way, even were there sufficient books to do so. But it should happen whenever there are favourable opportunities and, in the absence of books at the right level, teachers can tell relevant stories rather than read them. Many years ago I read a fascinating historical novel about the life of Hannibal. It was far too complicated to read to primary school children but the knowledge which I had gained from it enabled me to tell stories about the famous general's battle tactics to ten-year olds who might otherwise have remembered him simply for his journey across the Alps.

Integrated story

Rather than find relevant stories to fit in with subjects, some teachers will be happier investigating how parts of the curriculum can be linked

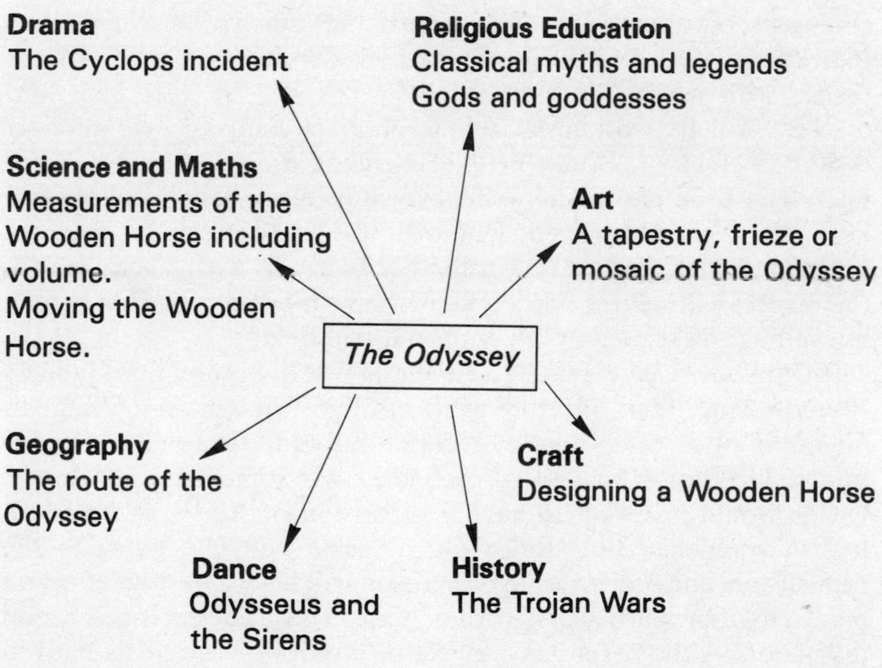

to a particular story. Taking Homer's Odyssey as an example, a web diagram could be constructed, as shown.

Obviously, there are many other possibilities, some of which will be determined by the age range of the pupils involved. Such work can, of course, be overdone. Used sparingly, it can add fresh purpose to story-telling and reading in an attractive way.

Story as therapy

Despite the dated nature of Katherine Cather's work and the apprehension which phrases such as 'Stories to develop or stamp out certain traits' arouse, it has frequently been claimed that story can help to change attitudes in a positive way. Dewey Chambers also discussed this, making use of a modern term – 'bibliotherapy'.

Bibliotherapy is a technique which attempts to help individuals understand or even resolve some of their problems. Situations and characters in fiction are presented, which children can identify with. How the fictional problems are solved might help individuals in their approach to real life difficulties.

At one level, bibliotherapy is a medical technique, used by psychologists who are skilled at identifying exactly what problems individuals have. It is likely that a considerable proportion of the people with whom the psychologists work will be disturbed. Few teachers will be working at this level. In seeking to help severely disturbed children, Bruno Bettelheim made use of traditional fairy tales. His example might well have influenced both teachers and librarians to examine the possibilities of this type of work and there are indications that they are now using books in this way. Their work in this respect will be less intense and, perhaps, more intuitive but as long as caution and sensitivity are applied it will be of use.

A Christmas Carol is surely a good example of how human kindness is worth more than uncaring avarice. Slight though Aesop's fables might be, pride often does go before a fall, and slow and steady, as opposed to foolish changes of pace, does win some races.

One would not want to have a succession of stories all based on human problems. But stories which tackle bullying, going to the dentist, loneliness, friendship or heroism will have a positive effect on many children, particularly if some time is set aside for small group discussion. Although it has been claimed that it is extremely hard to dislodge prejudiced attitudes which have been acquired in the home, some of the best work linking books and attitudes has been done in the area of racial prejudice when small group discussion has been used.

Death might seem a strange subject for children's books yet there are a number of useful publications such as, *Goodbye Max* by Holly Keller, *Granpa* by John Burningham and *A Taste of Strawberries* by Doris Buchanon which help children to cope with the sadness of loss.

Before anyone can discount this approach to bibliotherapy, or reading therapy as it is sometimes called, the following questions might be considered.

- Might *The Railway Children*, for all its Victorian, middle class background, illustrate how some of the difficulties confronting one-parent families can be tackled?
- Might *Gumble's Yard* by John Rowe Townsend depict a more modern example of resourceful children in a fix in an urban environment?
- Might *The Snow Day* by Ezra Jack Keats show, in a tacit way, multi-ethnic co-existence in an urban setting?
- Might *John Patrick, Norman Hennessy, The Boy Who Was Always Late* by John Burningham be a hilarious example of why adults should listen to children?

Great care needs to be exercised. Too much concentration on children's problems can stifle the positive aspects of their lives. The therapeutic powers of both realism and fantasy can be over stressed. Sensitivity is the watchword.

Teaching by story-telling

Like bibliotherapy, this is not a new idea, though it is one which is often neglected or forgotten. At a time when the curriculum is being subjected to a degree of uniformity, it might well be in danger once more.

Teaching by story-telling means rather more than linking story with areas or aspects of the curriculum. It means that, whenever possible, lessons should have a story-telling format. Many teachers do this frequently, realising that a good story can enliven lessons which might otherwise be an uninspired mixture of comments, questions and written work.

Teaching as story telling is the subject of a recent book by Kieran Egan. Writing in Canada, his fear is not that teaching might be engulfed by a National Curriculum but rather that it is threatened by the objectives approach to education. He sees teaching by story-telling as an alternative to teaching by objectives. I am not entirely convinced by his reasoning. The two approaches need not necessarily be at odds. Teachers can use a story-telling method and still retain objectives which they want pupils to achieve. Nor do I think that every lesson should be shaped around a story. Nevertheless, his opposition to behaviourism and systematic teaching heavily dependent upon developmental notions is impressive. Often, he alleges, fantasy in literature is accepted by children despite the fact that they have experienced nothing in real life which has prepared them for this. In other words, they have not moved from the concrete to the abstract. Story-telling might, in fact, be able to reverse this process.

Egan's framework for what might be termed the story lesson is attractive.

(1) He identifies what is important in a topic.
(2) He finds what he terms as binary opposites which will pinpoint the topic's implications.
(3) He organises the material into story form.
(4) He decides how to resolve and conclude the story.

It is the second point which is crucial. By selecting binary opposites Egan appears to be seeking to identify possible consequences in an either/or way. This is best illustrated by looking at some traditional tales.

- Will the wolf's cunning and wickedness overcome the third little pig's ingenuity and caution?
- Will Snow White's inherent goodness be a match for her stepmother's jealousy?

Similarly, to take an example from a children's classic,

- Will the alleged omniscience of the Wizard of Oz enable him to dispense with the afflictions of the Tin Man, the Scarecrow and the Cowardly Lion?

Clearly, from a story-telling aspect, the binary opposites involve negative and positive consequences and, as they are developed, shades of meaning.

Yet again, it is History and Religious Education which are best suited to this approach.

For a short time teaching by story-telling might appear bewildering as one struggles to find binary factors in Mathematics, Science, Art and Craft or Physical Education. But identifying binary opposites becomes relatively easy with practice. Here are some examples:

Addition	or	Subtraction	Drought	or	Rain
Drudgery	or	Convenience	Infection	or	Protection
Computation	or	Calculator	Sound	or	Silence
Accuracy	or	Estimation	Swiftness	or	Stealth

By making use of binary opposites it is possible to produce a story approach for most subjects in the primary curriculum. For instance, an unschooled giant might be pleased to learn from a wise old man that multiplying three gold sovereigns by 350 is just as accurate and much more quick than adding three gold sovereigns 350 times. Obviously, at times the binary opposites will not be so clear cut as some of the examples above. Nor will the conclusion always be immediately obvious or absolute. Most important, it is unlikely that teaching by story-telling will ever last a whole lesson. It is far more likely to be used as an introduction or as a conclusion.

We are, in fact, back to where we started. Many teachers know that a good story makes a lesson interesting. Although Egan's ideas are by no means infallible, it is well worth considering whether some lessons would be more interesting if they could be made into good stories. As skilled story-tellers, we should be able to do that.

Story and the National Curriculum

Early documents give Story more prestige than it has ever been afforded previously. There is no doubt whatsoever that both the telling and reading aloud of stories are treated with immense respect in the National Curriculum. It is particularly pleasing to note that these activities are not seen simply as items within the programme for Speaking and Listening: their contribution to Writing and Reading is also recognised. The following extracts provide examples.

> . . . listening and responding to stories
> . . . telling stories
> (*Programme of study for speaking and listening – key stage I – detailed provisions*)
>
> . . . regularly hear stories, told or read aloud
> (*Programme of study for reading – key stage 1 – general provisions*)
>
> . . . hear books, stories and poems read aloud or on radio, tape or television

> ... re-tell, re-read or dramatise familiar stories and poems.
> (*Programme of study for reading – key stage 1 – detailed provisions*)
>
> ... write in response to a range of well chosen stories
> (*Programme of study for writing – key stage 1 – detailed provisions*)
>
> ... listen attentively to stories and poems and talk about them
> (*Speaking and listening – statement of attainment – level 2*)
>
> ... listen and respond to stories, poems and other material read aloud, expressing opinions informed by what has been read.
> (*Reading – statement of attainment – level 2*)
>
> ... write stories showing an understanding of the rudiments of story structure
> (*Writing – statement of attainment – level 2*)

Just as useful are the suggestions in the section in the Non-Statutory Guidance which deals with planning schemes of work for Reading.

> Teachers should plan to:
> ... read aloud at least daily to the class or group from fiction ... adding new material but also re-reading old material. This should not be relegated to the end of the day.
>
> ... use stories on tape or video to give a further opportunity to choose another form of re-telling.
>
> ... use children's knowledge of stories, events, rhymes and jingles from other sources such as television or comics to develop an understanding of the different forms a story or account can take.
>
> ... use story-telling as an important way of introducing children to the enjoyment of narrative and including, in their experience, stories from oral traditions.

Summary

Story-telling and story-reading in the classroom should involve both children and a variety of adults, particularly parents and teachers and, if possible, professional story-tellers.

Children should not merely listen to stories, they should be able to tell them. Many of them can do this from an early age but the process can be accelerated by practice. Re-telling traditional tales is a most useful introduction to this work. Children who become effective tellers of tales are likely to find that their story-writing becomes more efficient as a result.

Telling and reading stories should not be confined to the language curriculum in the narrowest sense. Both activities can be linked to topics and specific school subjects.

The use of story is a means of making many lessons more interesting and effective.

A starter list of stories

INFANTS

The Hungry Giant	Wheaton Publishers
Peepo	Allan and Janet Ahlberg
Each Peach, Pear, Plum	Allan and Janet Ahlberg
Bears on Wheels	Stan and Jan Berenstein
The Snowman	Raymond Briggs*
The Very Hungry Caterpillar	Eric Carle
Watch Out – A Giant	Eric Carle
My Naughty Little Sister	Dorothy Edwards
Alfie Gets in First	Shirley Hughes
Rosie's Walk	Pat Hutchins
Not Now, Bernard	David McKee
The Snowy Day	Ezra Jack Keats
Lavinia's Cottage	John Goodall

* This is a book entirely without words. The pictures tell the story.

YOUNGER JUNIORS

The Wizard of Oz	L.Frank Baum
The Forest of Bowland Light Railway	B. B.
A Bear Called Paddington	Michael Bond
Father Christmas	Raymond Briggs
Maybe It's a Tiger	Kathleen Hershom
The Iron Man	Ted Hughes
Stig of the Dump	Clive King
Just So Stories	Rudyard Kipling
The Battle of Bubble and Squeak	Phillipa Pearce
Farmer Giles of Ham	J. R. R. Tolkien
The Little House in the Big Woods	Laura Ingalls Wilder

OLDER JUNIORS

Break in the Sun	Bernard Ashley
The Children of Green Knowe	Lucy Boston
Danny, Champion of the World	Roald Dahl
The Wind in the Willows	Kenneth Grahame
The Turbulent Term of Tike Tiler	Gene Kemp
Emil and the Detectives	Erich Kastner
The Railway Children	E. Nesbit
The King of the Golden River	John Ruskin
Treasure Island	Robert Louis Stevenson
The Horned Helmet	Henry Treece
Antelope Singer	Ruth Underhill
Charlotte's Webb	E. B. White

Favourite legends and folk tales

The Classical Legends
Norse Legends
Tales of Robin Hood
Arthurian Legends
Aesop's Fables
Folk tales from India
Africa and the East
Brer Rabbit and Anansi stories.

Favourite collectors of fairy tales, myths and legends

Andrew Lang
George McDonald
Joseph Jacobs
Rudyard Kipling
Ruth Manning Saunders
Barbara Leonie Picard
Kathleen Lines
Eileen Colwell
Ralph Lavender
Keith Crossley-Holland
The Brothers Grimm
Hans Andersen
Charles Perrault
Roger Lancelyn-Green

References

Baker, A. and Greene, E. (1977) *Storytelling: Art and Technique*. Bowker.

Cather, K. D. (1919) *Education by Story Telling*. Harrap and Co.

Chambers, D. W. (1971) *Children's Literature in the Curriculum*. Rand McNally.

Colwell, E. (1980) *Storytelling*. Bodley Head.

Egan, K. (1988) *Teaching as Storytelling*. Routledge.

Fox, C. and Dombey, H. (1986) 'Shared Experience', *Times Educational Supplement*, 21 Nov.

Jones, G. (1980) 'The effect of reading on changing children's attitudes', *Links* Vol. 5, No. 3.

Reed, D. (1990) *101 Good Read-Alouds*. Reading and Language Information Centre, Reading University.

Rosen, H. and Rosen, C. (1973) *The language of primary school children*. Penguin.

Rubin, R. J. (1978) *Using Bibliotherapy – A guide to theory and practice*. Oryx Press.

Sandell, P. *et al*. (1988) 'Story-telling', *Child Education*, June.

Shedlock, M. (1951) *The Art of the Storyteller*. Dover Publications.

Trelease, J. (1984) *The Read-Aloud Handbook*. Penguin.

Wade, B. (1984) 'Story at Home and at School', *Educational Review*, Occasional Publications.

Wells, G. (1987) *The Meaning Makers*. Hodder and Stoughton.

Acknowledgements

Kath Ahern for reference to 'Developing Story in the Infant School'. Unpublished dissertation, Department of Education, Liverpool Polytechnic, 1987.

Rita Bibby for extracts from 'Developing Story'. Unpublished dissertation, Department of Education, Liverpool Polytechnic, 1987.

Jeanette Galloway, Paula Marie Kelly, Sarah Jackson, for transcripts of children's story-telling.

Useful information

The National Community Folktale Centre, Middlesex Polytechnic, All Saints, White Hart Lane, London, N17 8HR: provides a list of storytellers, price £1.

CHAPTER 3

Responding to Literature

Response to literature is presently developing very quickly. The principal reason for this sudden and rapid development lies in the current approaches to the teaching of reading. Learning how to read and reading for pleasure are not now regarded as consecutive activities. Primary pupils no longer make use of 'readers' and reading schemes before progressing to story books. Both activities go on at the same time. And reading schemes no longer consist of books which are dull and unattractive. As much as possible, they resemble normal books. Nor do pupils progress painstakingly from one lengthy graded reader to the next. Instead, they are likely to read as many as a dozen short attractive books which are all at the same level. Rather than taking a week or more to finish a reader, they might well be completing four or five short books in the same time.

Modern approaches to reading have encouraged a resurgence of the 'Real Book' movement. If graded readers are increasingly being made to resemble mainstream fiction why not go the whole hog and dispense with graded readers? The most successful advocates seem to be those who are the most careful. Liz Waterland, for example, seems to combine the approach with a considerable amount of structured reading instruction. Some other experiments have been less successful.

Whether one approves of the notion of relying on Real Books or not, a related idea is certainly attractive. Right from the start reading is now seen as a quest for meaning. Understanding the story is more important than simply decoding words. Hence, hearing children read is now a much more thought-out activity which actively encourages pupils to respond positively to their reading material. Attitudes to reading are treated with more importance and more time is allowed for silent reading.

Response to literature is developing rapidly because there are far more opportunities for response to occur.

Theory to practice

Much has been written on the subject of children's response to literature. A great deal of it is theoretical and, to some extent, tentative for fairly obvious reasons. It is possible to ask children what they think about books: their written and oral answers will help us to understand, in a generalised way, how they respond to such questions. Trying to work out what goes on in their heads during or immediately after they have been reading is another matter. At best we obtain what Michael Benton terms introspective recall – that is, the child's ideas about written material immediately after it has been read.

Benton makes use of two theories which are attractive, educated and eminently respectable guesses about the nature of the encounter between children and books. The first is J. R. R. Tolkien's description of a secondary world which children enter when they read fantasy. The rules and conventions of the real world must be suspended if such stories are to be appreciated and made intelligible. Thus, fantasy is rarely discarded even by pupils who know very well that what they read is idealistic and impossible. Surely, most of us are willing to enter this secondary world even when we grow up? James Bond, Rocky and ET are not of the real world. Ebenezer Scrooge's overnight conversion from miser to philanthropist is unlikely, as are some of the coincidences in Dickens's finest work.

Most pre-school children fail to distinguish between the real and the secondary world when they listen to stories. Another interesting commentator on response, Arthur Applebee, has produced evidence which shows that at the age of six many children do not realise that fairy stories do not deal with real events, whereas by the time they are nine almost all of them are able to identify the difference between fact and fiction. It is, I suppose, rather like the difference between believing in Father Christmas and merely wanting to believe in him.

The second idea quoted by Benton, and many other investigators concerned with response, is D. W. Harding's 'onlooker' theory. According to Harding a reader can become so involved in a story that it is seen through the eyes of a character: a role is assumed and identified with. Despite this, the onlooker can never become an active participant who changes the events. We can see this very clearly by observing pupils in classrooms and playgrounds. Even the most extroverted child-actor who steals attention away from those with major parts in the class play can only go so far. Otherwise the play will lose its original meaning. Goldilocks is Goldilocks is Goldilocks! Out in the playground Batmen, Wonderwomen and Supermen abound. There they are at liberty to interpret their roles more widely than in a play. Either the participants accept this, there is some compromise, or some leave and new players are found. Yet the 'stories' will be very similar because the main characters behave in accepted ways. Wonderwoman does not rob banks.

This does not imply that children must completely accept the dictates of plot and character. Applebee differentiates between *objective response*, which depends on the strategic information supplied by the writer, and *subjective response*, which relies upon the individual reader's interpretation of what the writer has not made explicit. For example, in the Odyssey, Polyphemus is undoubtedly a one-eyed giant. Whether he is cruel or pathetic, or both, depends upon individual interpretation. He might be reviled by the reader, or pitied.

So far, so good. We can envisage primary school pupils moving from a world where the read and told are accepted with almost absolute belief to another where fact and fiction are differentiated but where the rational structure of everyday life is knowingly suspended in order to indulge in the world of fantasy. We can appreciate that children are not passive recipients of fiction: stories are open to interpretation. Thereafter, response theory tends to become more complex.

Arthur Applebee provides evidence which indicates that even at the age of two many children have picked up the traditional story-telling mode at its most basic. By the time most of them are five they can identify traditional beginnings and make consistent use of the past tense although some of them still have difficulty with story endings. Yet despite this impressive ability, young children find it difficult to evaluate stories. When they try, they usually repeat the story as best they can or refer to isolated incidents. Older primary pupils aged between seven and 11 are more likely to be able to summarise a story and to explain what it is about, but it is unusual for them to analyse plots or characters save in a very subjective way. Robert Protherough reinforces this contention. Even older primary pupils, he claims, judge a book mainly by whether they like it or not or, advancing slightly further, by whether they find the subject attractive. Thus a book might be deemed good by a young Liverpool supporter because it was about football.

What does all of this imply for classroom practice? Protherough has identified what he has called 'the broken-backed curriculum' in English teaching. In the primary school children respond in an individual way to books, armed mainly with enthusiasm and the ability to listen and read. At secondary level, although this is changing now, response still tends to be stylised and very much influenced by teachers' ideas and the requirements of external examinations. Until recently there seems to have been little continuity or logical progression.

In the primary school we may have to accept a framework whereby we encourage children's intuitive ability to tell stories. We also need to encourage them to interpret stories for themselves yet not prescribe excessive probing by too complicated means. Nor should we stray too far away from the story in our endeavours to develop response. Protherough uses another interesting term – 'curriculum spring-boarding'. It refers to a tendency to make literature a jumping-off point for other subjects and topics. Admittedly, definition in this respect can become blurred in the flurry of classroom life. Some readers might not regard a number of the activities described further on in this chapter as being particularly relevant to the teaching of literature; others might applaud them. Nevertheless, most would probably agree that it would not be entirely satisfactory for *Treasure Island* to be used merely as an introduction to a study of the Caribbean or for *The Silver Sword* to be little more than a lead in to a project about refugees.

It is hoped that the framework provided will be useful. The danger is that some of the theories on which it is based are distinctly developmental. We have to avoid accepting these theories as exact. Clearly, you will makc littlc preogress if you ask most four-year olds why they like particular books. The response is likely to be of a 'hole in my bucket' kind.

> 'Why do you like this book?'
> 'Because it is nice'
> 'Why is it nice?'
> 'Because I like it'
> 'Why do you like this book?' . . . .

But who can say for certain that the sensitive use of a number of strategies will not help to develop children's response to books? Evidence that primary children have difficulty in understanding plot and character is not really a valid excuse for doing nothing about it.

Donald Fry provides some excellent examples of what can happen after only a few conversations about books between teachers and individual children. Clayton, aged eight and in need of remedial reading assistance, became the class authority on *Watership Down*. Becoming an authority – on *Watership Down*, *A Christmas Carol*, *The Bongleweed*, *Roger the Razor Fish*, *Carrie's War*, Edward Lear, E. M. Nesbit, Enid Blyton or Babette Cole – is probably what response to literature is all about.

The nature of response

An experienced teacher of English was catching a bus home. The driver recognised her. 'You read *Wind in the Willows* to us,' he said. 'I didn't like it then but it was on the television a few weeks back.' The bus was due to depart and other passengers were waiting to pay, otherwise the conversation might have been lengthier and more erudite. But the Loch Ness Monster had surfaced.

Readers are entitled to an explanation of that last, apparently idiosyncratic, statement. Michael Benton, an interesting commentator on the subject, has likened children's response to literature to the monster of the Loch. You never see it, you think it is there and continue to search in the hope that you will eventually catch a glimpse. My own feeling is that response is more like an iceberg: nine-tenths of it is submerged but some of it is always in evidence.

By what means do children respond to fiction? They might

- think about it
- talk about it
- write bout it
- respond in some visual way as an alternative to writing.

It is the thought factor which creates most difficulties. To begin with children are not always willing to share their thoughts with others. Often they choose what they want to reveal rather like the boy in Jan Mark's book *Thunder and Lightnings* who churned out project after project about fish rather than communicate his real interests to his teachers. Response might sometimes be secret. And children are adept from an early age at telling teachers what they want to know rather than what they, the children, think. And, of course – to return to our bus driver – response can be long term.

We hope to sow the seeds of long-term response in our pupils. It is not unusual for many adults to remember books which interested them at school. Even Desperate Dan evokes a nostalgia in many adults, some of whom do not allow their own children to read comics. As teachers, however, it is the short term response that we are mainly concerned with. We seek to encourage it so that it can be developed. We evaluate it and hope that this will help us to inspire an interest in books which will last for life.

The silent response

I wish to make a plea for the avoidance of developing response to fiction ad nauseam. As this chapter will indicate, strategies to assist children to react to the books which they read are now in great abundance. '24 things to do', '25 teacher tested ways' . . . the lists of suggestions go on and on, leaving both pupils and teachers reeling from the impact. Response to literature is dependent on reading. If there is not time for that, then children might well be responding to activities rather than books. Too many questions to test their understanding of the text are likely to cause irritation. The silent response is not a contradiction of terms. It is something which should be respected.

The key to understanding about today's classroom practice probably lies in what used to happen. At one time, reading fiction ranked third in terms of prestige when compared to writing and comprehension in the primary curriculum. Children read stories and had books read to them but what they thought about them did not seem to be very important. Perhaps this reflected the approach to teaching in many secondary schools. What the children thought about the book did not really matter: it was up to the teacher to tell the child what to think. The consequences of this have often been disastrous. A number of investigations have shown that as they approach the examination years many secondary pupils read only what they have to. Even earlier than that, the number of books read voluntarily is small, and in primary schools many children are proficient at reading without really enjoying it. In a Schools' Council Survey published in 1981 Vera Southgate asked a number of primary pupils why they learned how to read. The reply of one young man was 'So you can stop.'

Secondary school approaches have changed. Pouring facts into pupils' heads was to some extent responsible for the decline in popularity of English Literature as an examination subject. For a number of years now children have been encouraged to develop their own ideas. This has happened in primary schools also.

Response to what?

Of course, it is response to books which we are mainly encouraging. But why shouldn't it also be response to newspapers, magazines, and even comics? Comics, it might be claimed, are at the very heart of many children's reading. Shouldn't we also be encouraging response to films, stories on television, audio and video cassettes?

We might even ask 'Response to whose books?' In asking that question I am staking a claim for two forms of literature which have become much more important in recent years. They are stories written by pupils and their teachers. Donald Graves, perhaps the major force in the process approach to children's writing, has claimed that children's best efforts at writing should take the form of books, attractively bound and illustrated, which might at times even be word processed. These works should be in class libraries alongside more commercial productions.

We have already seen that teachers' versions of local folk tales are attractive to their pupils. As they gain in confidence many teachers branch out, writing interesting stories about haunted schools, ghosts in cellars, talking cars with minds of their own, original fairy tales and even pop-up books. Classroom authors, young and old, are worth responding to.

Encouraging response

In order to encourage response we can make use of a whole variety of activities which are dependent on reading fiction. One of the earliest examples of this approach is provided by the Open University book *Children, Language and Literature*. In one large section of the book a host of ideas are put together. One of the best known articles is Geoff Fox's '24 things to do with a book'. Keeping logs, character descriptions, poster and cover designs, authors in schools, visual displays, re-telling stories on tape and taking on roles are some examples of how books can be discussed, written about and represented in other forms. In other parts of this section, initial reactions to chapters are advocated, effective role playing is described and there is an account of one very effective small group discussion; groups reading to one another, plot-prediction and an intriguing description of a story celebration involving a project which culminated in a visit by Helen Cresswell, to the Grand Pie Contest.

A number of other lists have since appeared and there are times when the compilers seem to be struggling to retain originality: providing good reasons why a monster which has invaded your bedroom should not destroy your favourite book is an idea which has cropped up on several occasions.

The examples provided in *Children, Language and Literature* are probably quite sufficient for most teachers who wish to make a start with this type of work. With a little experience they will begin to devise their own alternatives. A crossword puzzle based on a book and a booklet which encourages children to create their written and artistic impressions of Winnie the Pooh are two recent examples of ideas tried out by teachers in training.

Other more generalised methods of encouraging response include organising Book Clubs, Book Weeks and library visits. Book Weeks are not unlike the Story Festivals described in Chapter 2 and the Poetry Festivals which will be discussed in Chapter 5. It might appear that the curriculum could become overloaded with fiction festivals of one sort or another but any one of the three mentioned above can include the other two.

In a more general way, encouraging response depends very much on the establishment of a reading environment within and beyond the classroom. Are there enough books available? Are there sufficient opportunities for them to be read? Are books satisfactorily displayed and publicised? Does the reading environment extend beyond the provision of books? Are magazines and comics available? What about newspapers? Is there a tape bank? Can videotapes be seen regularly? Are there comfortable reading places and is the reading environment linked to public libraries and individual homes? In other words is response being encouraged in an enthusiastic way? Is reading a popular activity?

Developing response

The activities described usually excite children, particularly if they are unused to having fiction treated in this way. Suddenly, an increased interest in fiction seems to spark off a whole variety of activities. Systematic planning is needed, however, if enthusiasm, spontaneity and inventiveness are to produce useful results. Taking part in fiction-related activities should help our pupils to develop a deeper understanding of the material which they read. For this to happen we need to identify the essential approaches to developing response, at the same time recognising the value of more ephemeral ones which will help get the process working. Talking about fiction, dramatising it, writing about it and representing it in some artistic way include most of the essential ingredients.

Talking about books is thought to be almost as useful as reading aloud when it comes to improving children's reading ability. Might it be that discussion promotes understanding which in turn makes a text more interesting? This sort of work is usually at its best when it involves small group discussion. In Chapter 5 the mechanics of this arrangement are discussed in detail. At this stage it is sufficient to say that within groups of three to five everyone will have an opportunity to talk. This usually makes the arrangement much more productive than conventional whole-class discussions.

Small group discussions, or reading conferences as they are often called in America, are extremely useful with young children. Usually, the teacher takes part, encouraging the rest of the group to talk about their interests, likes and dislikes, and opinions. With older children the teacher is not required although in the initial stages some ground rules need to be set in terms of what is to be discussed. The effectiveness of the story, plots, characters, language and meaning are the most usual topics although a book might be examined for one specific factor. For example, Raymond Briggs's *Fungus the Bogeyman* might be examined to find out how the Bogey world reverses the values of everyday life. Similarly, *Where the Wild Things Are* might stimulate a discussion about the negative and positive qualities of monsters.

Oral work must also involve dramatic approaches. Allowing children to act out and improvise scenes from books encourages greater understanding. Placing them in the position of various characters will do the same. There is also what is termed the 'hot seat' approach in which pupils adopt the role of a character whose actions and behaviour have to be explained to the rest of the group. A number of publications intended for secondary school pupils take a variety of texts and suggest that they can be interpreted by children working in pairs. There seems to be no reason why such work cannot be adopted for the primary school. Recently, watching several pairs of eight year olds working out the best way of reading Roger McGough's haunting poem 'First Day at School', I learned from them how it really should be read, perhaps because all of these children were more capable of simulating a faltering, five-year old voice than I was. At another level, twenty top infants acting out their version of *Where the Wild Things Are* would be worth watching.

If there is a danger about written response it is that children probably write too much already. So what is asked of them needs to be stimulating and imaginative. Writing might be attractively linked to character study. Take, for example, John Ruskin's lucid portrayal of the South West Wind in human guise in his story *The King of the Golden River*. Can it help children to achieve clarity in their character descriptions? Might listing the positive and negative qualities of Long John Silver in Stevenson's *Treasure Island* help them to understand that fictional characters, like their real life counterparts, are not straightforward? Younger children will undoubtedly be interested in the pictorial portrayal of character and can be encouraged to comment on it.

Visual representation of fiction appeals to most children. It might be used to develop their sense of sequence or to show how they interpret the incidents and characters which they encounter in fiction. Collages, friezes, models and maps can all be used for these purposes.

In Chapter 2 we saw how projects can be centred on a story. This has become a marked tendency in recent years. In some cases the greater part of the language programme for a particular class is concentrated for considerable periods of time on one book. This kind of work was pioneered by Bretton Hall College and Wakefield LEA in the early part of this decade and has continued to develop since then. A recent example is provided by *Using Books in the Classroom* by Hazel Short. Here an impressive range of fiction is used to develop a wide variety of activities with groups of varying size. It is noticeable that all of the books are good ones. They include *The Iron Man*, *The Hobbit*, *The Wheel on the School* and more recent books of quality such as *The Bongleweed* by Helen Cresswell and *The Great Piratical Rumbustification* by Margaret Mahy. Quality is a crucial factor in this approach. If we are to spend fairly lengthy amounts of time working with literature then it is important that it should be good.

Yet another book which has become very popular is *Into Books – 101 Literature Activities in the Classroom* by Ron Thomas and Andrew Perry. Work is provided for three different age levels, 5–7, 8–9 and 10–12. Each of these is preceded by a framework which lists activities, teaching points and the use of appropriate literary forms. In this respect it represents a remarkable forecast of the National Curriculum. Much of the work is based on themes and sensibly includes lists of books which can be used to develop them. Another alternative is to take a particular book and develop activities chapter by chapter. Both approaches can help children to a better understanding of fiction.

Concentration upon one book raises a problem which is not uncommon in primary schools. Whereas in the secondary sector there are still many sets of books available for class study, the emphasis at primary level has been on single copies of a large number of books. Providing 20 or more copies of one book can be expensive and, of course, is likely to diminish the amount of money available for library stock. Co-operative book schemes might provide an answer to this problem. A group of schools, for instance, could decide which books they might wish to study in detail. They could join together to purchase them so that a centralised stock could gradually be built up. In addition, a number of publishers are now conscious of literature links with language and are making sets of books and suggestions for their use available at sensible prices.

Provided that teachers possess a good working knowledge of the best fiction available, the books and articles mentioned should provide a very firm basis for encouraging and developing response. Experience of this sort of work indicates that teachers constantly modify and adjust ideas to suit their own working environment. Furthermore, when pupils become involved in literature based work it is not unusual for them to suggest alternative activities to those provided by teachers or external sources. When this occurs, response is really beginning to develop.

It is, of course, the ideas which individual teachers are encouraged to develop which moves this work along. Other people's ideas are all very well but they have to be adapted to suit the needs of particular groups and individuals. Consequently, looking at work in progress in familiar classrooms, coupled with the ideas discussed with teachers who are seeking for new approaches to response, are often the sources of much inspiration.

The linking of art and craft work to response has already been mentioned. This approach is absolutely vital for work with young children. There is far more to drawing and painting than meets the eye. Recently *The Lion, the Witch and the Wardrobe* was introduced to a class of top infants. This is a challenging book for pupils in this age group yet they responded with enthusiasm. Little writing was produced. But there was a great deal of work in pictorial form. The pictures were by no means uniform. Obviously the characters were common to most drawings but their activities varied according to the episode chosen by each individual. Most impressive was the willingness and ability of these children to talk about their drawings. Although they might have had difficulty in writing about *The Lion, the*

Witch and the Wardrobe they certainly knew a lot about it. Talking about pictures was talking about the book.

Drama, which has been considered already, can produce similar results. Children, like actors, will interpret plot and character as they act out stories; evidence acquired recently reinforces the effectiveness of this approach. Children who comment in writing about particular characters in a book tend to consider the obvious; their descriptions of people, for example, are usually related to dress and appearance. Following dramatisation there is often a marked change. Personality, motives and emotions are taken into account to a much greater extent.

With all of this work one has to be wary of the spring-boarding effect mentioned by Protherough in research discussed earlier in this chapter. In a fairly recent book Joyce Moss focuses on literature by selecting books on a particular topic. Following serialised readings children are encouraged to consider genre, character, setting and the book's basic plot. The work is adapted to the ages of the pupils involved. In some ways it is not unlike the approach taken by Ron Thomas and Andrew Perry but the insistence on returning to the same questions time and again is too close to interrogation by plot for my liking. The enthusiasm for story-telling is obvious but might there be some spring-boarding in the direction of literary criticism?

Having said that, it was refreshing to see the turn taken by a useful approach to classical legends. A class of third year juniors were being introduced to Homer's *Iliad*. This in itself was useful: the classic legends are too often neglected. Following a discussion of the role of the story-teller in ancient Greece, the story was serialised. Each episode was introduced formally as though the audience were Greeks of long ago. Not surprisingly much art work and modelling resulted. The enthusiasm of the teacher was such that her pupils were eager to write at length about what they were learning. When they were asked how it was possible to find out all that they knew about the *Iliad* most of these children were quite certain what the solution was: surprisingly they requested to have a written test. Had the teacher imposed this, one wonders what the result would have been. Yet this group wrote enthusiastically in answering a number of questions written on the blackboard. One can never be absolutely certain about children – or the form which their response will take.

Evaluating response

Talking about books can be evaluated by scrutinising transcripts, by listening in to discussions and by making notes about individual contributions. Dramatisation of fiction, writing and artwork can all have their worth estimated in terms of the quality of their communication. In short, this type of evaluation is what takes place in primary school classrooms already.

There is one further kind of evaluation which tends to be neglected. It involves the recording of what children actually read.

An examination of the records kept by the vast majority of primary schools would reveal a meticulous approach to the recording of children's progress while they are learning to read. Thereafter, record keeping tends to fall away. It is as if we think that once the basics have been mastered children can look after themselves and, just as long as they seem to be doing some reading, we have no need to probe. If I had needed to be convinced that children's fiction reading should be monitored the experience of one of my DASE course members would have provided me with ample evidence. As part of an assignment she kept track of the reading done by six of her ten-year old pupils over a period of four weeks. The members of this group were all slow readers who had struggled with their reading scheme. During the four weeks not one of them completed a book although they selected a considerable number from the library. Careful back-tracking revealed that it was unlikely that any books had been completely read by the group from the time that they had finished their reading scheme. Reading schemes and fiction were consecutive rather than concurrent activities in the school concerned and it is possible that had the reverse applied this group would not have been in such a parlous state. The Bullock Report pointed out how many pupils failed to realise that reading could be a pleasurable experience. In this respect, the time when they are coming off reading schemes is crucial. In my experience it takes no more than three or four unsuccessful selections for a child to regard reading as an experience which creates difficulty and failure. A lack of reading records means that this can happen without anyone really noticing. Having been alerted to the problem, this particular teacher introduced carefully selected books to the group and the situation improved. To quote Ronald Regan, her action had come 'just in time'.

Records will pinpoint consistent failure to complete books quite quickly, thereby enabling teachers to take positive action. But failure to complete books – or book rejection, as it is sometimes called – is not necessarily a negative action, provided that it does not happen too often. My own research suggests that top juniors rejected as many as one third of the books which they select – revealing perhaps a healthy approach to book selection. Adults often make errors when selecting books from libraries. If they do not enjoy books which they are reading for pleasure then they are unlikely to persevere with them. Why should children, whose powers of discrimination are inexperienced and less sharp, be expected to finish books which they do not like? The notion that children should finish all the books which they select is, I think, a mistaken one. Nevertheless, older junior children can improve their powers of selection so that failure is less likely. By looking at the summary of the story which is usually near the cover, examining the introduction and skimming through the book, selection mistakes tend not to happen so often.

The mention of records is enough to cause most primary teachers to shrug in resignation. How much more record keeping is needed? Surely the implementation of the National Curriculum is creating more than enough record keeping already? Yet keeping reading records need not be a particularly demanding task and it is certainly important.

What alternatives are there? One approach is the book review. Once a book has been completed, the reader provides a written account of what has been read. This is perfectly acceptable if the reader really wishes to do it. If there is a scheme whereby good books are publicised on a book board then many readers will be only too willing to tell their fellow pupils the good news. But as a routine activity, completed week in week out, book reviews can deteriorate into drudgery. How many adults would be prepared to review all of the books which they read for pleasure? Overdone, book reviews might well put children off reading rather than encourage them.

At the other end of the scale teachers might simply record what books pupils have read. There need be little drudgery about this but the information provided might not be really adequate. Is there some halfway house between the demands of the book review and the deficiencies of records which reveal very little? Pupil maintained records might provide a solution.

What do we need to know about pupils' voluntary reading? Teachers will have their own ideas about this but there is a danger that questionnaires or record sheets can demand too much information some of which might not be particularly useful. Record sheets which are too involved will put children off. A good record sheet is one which can be filled in without difficulty. Useful information will be:

- The title of the book (or other reading material).

- The name of the writer.
- The date when the book was taken from the library.
- The date when it was returned to the library.
- Whether the book was completely read.
- Comments about the book.

A relatively brief set of details such as this can provide a great deal of information. We can learn which books and which authors are popular or unpopular. We can learn how long it takes for books to be read, what pupils think of books and whether or not they complete them. By scrutinising a number of those record sheets we can also determine the quantitative and qualitative nature of children's reading.

Most junior pupils can use this form of reading record without difficulty. Blank record sheets can be kept in a box and placed in another when completed. Some preliminary discussions need to take place. Children should be told that by using these sheets they are helping to work out how useful their libraries are. For many this will be their first experience of consumer consultation. My experience is that in the initial stages many children exploit the system. Comments about the books abound with remarks such as 'boring', 'soppy', 'daft', 'useless'. It is as though they are taking revenge for not being

Name : ________________
My book is called ________________________
My book was written by __________________

consulted before. After several weeks they settle down and produce constructive comments. Some teachers have claimed that the use of records like this actually encourages children to read more frequently.

Many older infants too will be able to cope with this kind of sheet. Those who experience difficulty with writing will need to have the form filled in for them. This does not necessarily mean that the teacher has to do this. Other children will be glad to oblige.

If a very basic response is all that is required then a simple sheet with visual approach and comic-style speech bubble (as illustrated) could be used. This example uses features attractive to children, and avoids likes and dislikes, which very young children have difficulty in dealing with. Young children might well become confused about whether they finish books or not because so much of their reading material is short, so such questions are best avoided. Many teachers will prefer to create their own record sheets.

For the youngest children in the primary school, records will need to be verbal. They will probably develop from the reading conferences mentioned earlier in this chapter and can easily be recorded on tape.

Compared to the exciting work which is linked to the encouragement and development of response, evaluation might

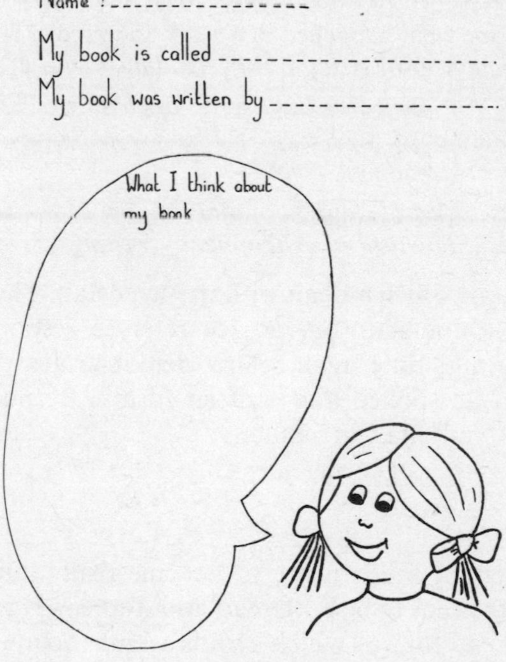

appear rather mundane. Yet the information which can be extracted from such records is invaluable. The pattern of a child's reading can be traced throughout the primary school. It might reflect the teacher intervention which will result from surveys of the record sheets. It should also mirror the effects of the sustained reading which is described in detail in the following chapter. Children are more likely to take a positive approach to reading and literature if they can see their success recorded in this way. Parents will also be impressed and I suspect that there is no better way of convincing Her Majesty's Inspectorate that literature is thriving in primary schools than to maintain a comprehensive record of what has been read.

Response and the National Curriculum

Not surprisingly, the National Curriculum abounds in advice and requests for encouraging and developing children's response to literature. For example,

> ... listen attentively to stories and poems and talk about them (*Statement of Attainment – speaking and listening – level 2*)
>
> ... relate real or imaginary events in a connected narrative which conveys meaning to a group of pupils, the teacher or another known adult. (*Statement of Attainment – speaking and listening – level 3*)
>
> ... describe what happened in a story and predict what might happen next. (*Statement of Attainment – reading – level 2*)
>
> ... bring to their writing and discussion about stories some understanding of the way stories are structured. (*Statement of Attainment – reading – level 3*)
>
> ... write stories showing an understanding of the rudiments of story structure. (*Statement of Attainment – writing – level 2*)

There is no topic which is dealt with in such detail. The programmes of study and the non-statutory advice refer to response indirectly or directly time and time again. This demonstrates the versatility of response and its spoken and written forms. Response to literature pervades the National Curriculum.

Summary

If primary school children are to become really interested in books then literature needs to be both read and studied. This must be done in a relaxed but careful way which avoids asking too much or making the task too scholarly. Teachers should take account of the research which is available in this respect. In particular, children's ability to tell stories should be encouraged and teachers should talk to individual children about the books which they are reading as much as possible.

A great many ways of encouraging and developing children's interest in fiction have been explored in recent years. From them teachers can select those which they think will best encourage the oral, written, dramatic and artistic responses of their pupils. Evaluation has a crucial role to play in this.

References

Applebee, A. (1978) *The Child's Concept of Story*. University of Chicago Press.

Benton, M. (1978) 'Children's Response to Stories'. *Children's Literature in Education* **10**, 2.

Benton, M. and Fox, G. (1987) *Teaching Literature – Nine to Fourteen*. Oxford University Press.

Bretton Hall College Language Development Unit and Wakefield LEA (1981) *Fiction as a starting point for learning 8–14* and *Fiction based English in the Middle School*.

C.A.C.E. (1975) *A Language for Life*. (The Bullock Report) HMSO.

Fenwick, G. (1975) 'Junior School Pupils' Rejection of Fiction Books'. *Educational Reseach,* **17**, 2.

Fox, G. (1987) '24 Things to do with a Book' in Hoffman *et al. Children, Language and Literature*. Open University Press.

Fry, D. (1985) *Children Talking about Books – Seeing themselves as readers*. Open University Press.

Graves, D. (1983) *Writing – Children and Teachers at Work*. Heinemann.

Moss, J. F. (1984) *Focus Units in Literature*. National Council of Teachers in English.

Short, H. (1989) *Using Books*. Scholastic Publications.

Southgate, V. (1981) *Extending Beginning Reading*. Heinemann.

Thomas, R. and Parker, A. (1989) *Into Books*. Oxford University Press.

Acknowledgements

Linda Todd for the cartoons in the reading records.

David Savage for ideas on shared sets of books.

Sue Sproson, Sue Brierley, Julie Jones and Eileen Holden for their stories.

Chris Vaudrey, Eileen Holden, Marjorie McConlough, Shirley Barnett, for their work on developing response.

Jean Barnes for her story about the bus driver.

CHAPTER 4

Time to Read

You might have a library brimming with attractive, interesting books. Alternatively, you might have one in which the stock is sparse and worn out. Most school and class libraries are somewhere in between these extremes. Yet unless one important condition is fulfilled the number of books in school makes not one scrap of difference. For books are of little use unless they are being read. And that implies that time has to be set aside for reading.

Silent reading in times past

Silent reading is a deceptively modern mass activity. Long ago, when books were created by hand they were both rare and expensive. Very few people must have been able to read the Lindisfarne Gospels at the time of their creation. But then at that time very few people were able to read.

Beyond the abbey walls in those days the wealthy owners of books were used to being entertained by strolling players and minstrels. They had books read to them and hence had little incentive to read for themselves. The story of how Alfred's mother promised the future king a valuable book once he could read it is remarkable mainly because Alfred's action was exceptional for the times.

Even with the invention of the printing press, books were still a luxury denied to the vast majority. The only one seen by most people would be the Holy Bible and it was often chained to the lectern. Clearly, the amount of silent reading which can be done is dependent upon both the amount of reading material available and its accessibility.

The Industrial Revolution and the subsequent move towards mass literacy created a much greater demand for books. Even then, books were still in short supply and a great deal of sharing had to be done in both school and home. This encouraged the oral tradition. As Laurie Lee shows, this was still very much in evidence in the early 1920s.

> Many a winter's night we would settle round the lamp-lit kitchen, after supper had been cleared away, while our mother took down one of her 'Penny' volumes and read to us by the hour.

As we have already seen, family reading still has much to commend it, but one can hardly say the same for the methods by which Laurie Lee had to pursue his quest for literacy. Here are some further examples of the future writer's experiences.

> I was at the village school when I read these books (*Pilgrim's Progress*, *Robinson Crusoe* and *Gulliver's Travels*) having bought the three of them at a rummage sale for a penny. At the school itself there were very few books, except things about Cats and Mats, or terse little pamphlets stating that Jill was Ill or Jack had broken his Back.
>
> On my way home from school I developed a special technique: at several pages a day while loitering at the bookstall at Woolworth's, I found I could read most of their stock in a year.
>
> Then suddenly, by chance, I stumbled on Dickens, finding his *Collected Works* on a bonfire.

Twenty years later, my own childhood reading depended very much upon the Beano and Dandy comics, and the collection of myths, legends, poetry and novels in the big mahogany bookcase in our front room; but most of all on the rich variety of literature gleaned by my parents from salerooms and jumble sales. Very few children's books were published during the Second World War and many of those already in existence failed to survive the onslaught of frequent waste paper campaigns. At school books were in extremely short supply and class readers were the order of the day.

When I started to teach in the late fifties, conditions had scarcely improved. School libraries had begun to have a small number of new books added to them each year but class libraries, where these existed, often consisted of a cupboard of elderly books, many of them backed with brown paper. The main worry was not so much the quality of the reading material but whether it would be adequate enough to last out the school year.

It was only in the mid-sixties that the book supply in schools really improved, mainly because of the rapid expansion of the paperback market. It was a time when there were more books in schools than ever before. Moreover, they were also more readily available to families and, as central heating became more common, more homes were able to provide a variety of suitable places in which they could be read. Unfortunately, by that time silent reading had been overtaken by a number of events. At home the number of activities competing for time increased. And at school silent reading was beginning to fall into disrepute.

The decline of silent reading

There were a number of reasons for silent reading's loss of popularity. The most notable ones were:

- an expanding curriculum;
- new teaching methods;
- changes in classroom design;
- the paramountcy of oral reading;
- lack of structure in silent reading activities;
- loss of professional faith.

The primary school curriculum was, and still is, changing rapidly. Arithmetic has been replaced by Mathematics, English has become Language Studies, Science has become much more important and, like Art and Craft, has developed links with Technology. Dance, Drama and Gymnastics jostle with Industrial Education and Integrated Studies for allocations of time within the school week. Is it any wonder that it has become harder to find a place for silent reading?

Many of the subjects mentioned above imply activity rather than passive learning. This reflects a pedagogical philosophy which has been gaining ground for many years. 'Activity' and 'discovery' methods have tended to make silent reading appear to be prosaic and unexciting. This does not have to be the case. As we shall see, it can be an exciting, invigorating activity; and it is a most useful instrument of much discovery in school and elsewhere.

Twenty years ago, open plan schools were very much in vogue. Today many schools have modified versions of the original concept. Experience has shown that modification was necessary. Whatever one's opinion about open-plan design – and I have always welcomed the move away from the relative isolation of the walled-in classroom – there is not much doubt that the early versions created difficulties for activities like silent reading. Some children can become so absorbed with books that they are almost oblivious to what is going on around them. But for many others noise and movement are definite distractions. Today, the best open plan schools have semi-enclosed areas, usually carpeted, for the purpose of quiet study.

There are, however, three more powerful and overlapping factors which have contributed to the decline of silent reading. One of them is its general lack of development in this country. Teachers of young children obviously require expertise in the teaching of reading. Much of this work is centred around oral practice, the sounding out of syllables, words, phrases and sentences. Certainly this is an important part of the process of learning to read but it has possibly been overdone. There has, perhaps, been too much sound and not enough silence. After all, once there is a reasonable supply of printed material available to the general public, what is the most common mode of reading? To read a newspaper aloud in a railway carriage would be regarded as eccentric and irritating.

Over-emphasis on oral reading in the early stages has, I think, contributed greatly to the neglect of silent reading. Its importance has been recognised for at least 50 years in the United States where it has been the subject of much research. Here, until recently, it has been regarded as something which takes care of itself once children have mastered the basic reading skills.

Lack of development is linked with lack of structure. Some years ago an Infant school teacher told me about her colleagues' response to her proposal for a fresh, ordered approach. 'They said it was just good old-fashioned silent reading modernised.'

They were right, of course. Methods and approaches in education fall in and out of fashion although the new version is never quite the same as the old.

In the past silent reading has often been presented in an unimaginative way, its use dubious. A. J. Jenkinson, who conducted one of the best known studies in children's reading interests in this country, identified defects as long ago as 1939. In a study of 28 Senior and Secondary schools (the pre-war equivalents of Secondary Modern and Grammar schools respectively) he discovered that the former were far more likely to encourage what he termed as 'quiet reading'. Closer inspection revealed that the reasons for this were not necessarily educational.

> For what is the origin of quiet reading in Senior schools? Does it spring from a greater sensitivity for enlightened modern tenets of education?

> No. It springs from two conditions under which Senior schools labour: lack of free periods and large classes. In such conditions teachers with all their marking and secretarial work manage free periods by allowing 'quiet reading'.

Almost two decades later, John Carsley hinted at similar conditions in primary schools. In a large-scale survey he found that pupils in urban and estate schools were allocated more time for silent reading than their counterparts in more favoured environments.

While efforts to improve the reading of less bright children and those in harsh environments can only be applauded, it does seem that often in the past silent reading has been used as a breathing space by hard-pressed teachers who needed some respite from the remorseless demands of large classes in difficult conditions. This goes a long way towards explaining the decline of silent reading and the suspicion and hostility which it has attracted in the not so distant past. Teachers, in fact, have often lost confidence. Lunzer and Gardner's Schools Council research in 1979 seems to confirm this.

> ... teachers regard reading in lesson time with some degree of suspicion. They feel uneasy if pupils are 'only reading': they consider they may be regarded as inefficient if a visitor to a lesson finds a substantial number of pupils merely gazing at books or resource materials.

The new approach

I first read about modern sustained reading in an article by Geoff Fox in the *Times Educational Supplement* in 1978. Until recently it has been the subject of only a few articles in this country, yet it has certainly captured the imagination of many teachers and is now practised in large numbers of schools.

The creation of what is usually termed 'USSR' is generally attributed to Dr Lyman C. Hunt of the University of Vermont. His theories were formulated, recorded and put into practice during the 1960s at a time when education on both sides of the Atlantic was undergoing major changes. By 1970 USSR was popular in both USA and Canada although it was some years before it was introduced in Great Britain.

The name of the game

There's a considerable number of alternative acronyms and names for

USSR. The following list is by no means exhaustive.

USSR	Uninterrupted Sustained Silent Reading, *or* Unified Sustained Silent Reading.
SSR	Sustained Silent Reading.
HIP	High Intensity Practice.
SQUIRT	Sustained Quiet Uninterrupted Intensive Reading Time.
SQIRT	Sssh, Quiet It's Reading Time.
USLAB	Uninterrupted Sustained Looking at Books.
SQWIB	Sitting Quietly with Interesting Books.
ERIC	Everybody Reads in Class.
DEAR	Drop Everything and Read.
	or
	Private Reading.
	Whole School Reading.
	Let the Children Read.

Whatever the name, the basic principles are the same. Whole School Reading and Unified Sustained Silent Reading usually imply that the activity is carried out simultaneously by all the pupils within a school.

Definition

Exactly what is USSR then? What makes it different from 'old fashioned silent reading'? The following definition (Fenwick, 1988) seems to cover what happens in most classrooms where it is practised.

> USSR is a structured form of silent reading. Pupils are given a set period of time for the activity and allowed a reasonable choice of reading material. Quietness is expected and interruptions discouraged. Formal testing of the activity is avoided.

Defined more closely than this, USSR becomes too prescriptive and does not allow for the varying conditions in individual schools and classrooms. Some of the early American definitions included references to procedures which indicated an alarming rigidity. For example,

> 50 minutes must be devoted to each session.
> Reading material must not be changed during that time.
> A timer or buzzer should be used to mark the commencement and completion of the activity.
> There should be absolute silence.

Happily, there is plenty of evidence to show that American teachers adapted these procedures to suit the needs of their own pupils while still adhering to basic principles. One should beware of being too sceptical of the restrictions mentioned above. The ideas of bells and buzzers to denote the start and finish of USSR is all rather too Skinnerian for me, yet an infant teacher has reported that one class of reception children regarded them as an important part of an agreeable game. Small groups actually played at USSR during lunch times and insisted on bringing their own alarm clocks. And I have met many older junior pupils who would have willingly read for 50 minutes and more.

How useful is USSR?

Before we embark upon an examination of the strategies which are needed when putting USSR into practice, it is essential that we should consider exactly what the activity might achieve. As we have seen, silent reading can be regarded with suspicion. Its justification, therefore, is vital. USSR can:

(1) allow pupils to practise silent reading for substantial periods of time;
(2) create conditions which allow for this type of reading to take place;
(3) give children an opportunity to read a wide range of reading material;
(4) increase children's motivation to read;
(5) help to improve reading skills.

The practice of silent reading is extremely important and has frequently been underrated. There is always a balance between learning skills and practising them. Young pianists, swimmers, skaters and tennis players all put in a great deal of work to achieve proficiency. In a similar way, reading might be likened to long distance running. An athlete becomes a good distance runner by running long distances. A reader develops reading competence, to some extent, by reading for long periods of time. There is something to be said for the acquisition of what might be termed 'reading stamina'.

Silent reading of this kind is more likely to be successful in quiet, comfortable conditions. The attention span of most primary school pupils is likely to be closely related to comfort in terms of seating, room temperature and noise levels. One would also assume that classroom practitioners who set up programmes of USSR will do their best to make certain that the supply of reading material is generous. By doing this they will be going some way to assuring that choice of material is fairly wide. And the more time pupils have for reading, the more versatile their reading is likely to be.

These justifications are based very much on common-sense and evidence culled from small-scale research both here and in the USA. The reader might well question the absence of the sort of conclusive evidence which extensive, in-depth research often provides. Its non-availability is not really surprising. Comparing the effects of USSR between schools and age groups would only be reliable if there was a high degree of uniformity in the procedures which were used. This is scarcely possible. Schools tend to adapt USSR to suit their own purposes and conditions.

Actual evidence will be discussed later in this chapter. Meanwhile, it seems reasonable to assume that the first three points listed above have been proved. Although programmes of USSR have occasionally been abandoned because of failure, the majority of reports show that it can be set up and practised effectively.

Many reports also comment on the improvement in attitudes which the activity seems to encourage. Evidence concerning the improvement of reading skills is less conclusive. Two issues might be borne in mind in this respect. First, USSR is in the great majority of cases only part of the reading programme. Hence it is difficult to make claims about what it does in terms of reading improvement in an isolated way. Second, it is likely that many teachers would not wish to measure USSR for this purpose.

Generally speaking, however, USSR does seem to be a successful activity. Had it not been, it would not have survived for so long. Its great strength is probably its potential to motivate children to enjoy reading. Many pupils regard it as the most useful part of the reading programme and look forward to it with enthusiasm.

Now that we have considered its possibilities and merits, the practical aspects of USSR need to be examined. This might best be done by posing a number of questions.

Can USSR be practised effectively with very young children?

USSR has sometimes been regarded as an activity which can only be used once children are reasonably proficient readers. I do not agree. It depends, of course, on how reading is defined, but I have seen it working with children in reception classes in infant schools, with extremely slow learners of junior age and with every age group at secondary level. Having recently discovered that only fifty per cent of a large group of students had heard of *The Wind in the Willows*, and that only half of these had actually read it, I am inclined to think that the introduction of USSR into Higher Education would be no bad thing.

If the first step towards literacy is picking up a book the right way up, then USSR can indeed be started at a very early age. There seems no reason why nursery children should not have their own version. Readers will have noted that an alternative acronym is USLAB – Uninterrupted Sustained Looking at Books. In my opinion, that is a valuable form of sustained reading. Nor should slow learners in the Primary school be excluded. We need to dispel the notion that reading disability precludes the use of books.

Is consultation important?

Even when a proposed programme is likely to take up very little time, it makes sense to consult a number of people.

Obviously, headteachers should be approached, as should language co-ordinators. Often they will need reassurance. USSR might well be competing for time and attention with paired, shared and individualised reading, and worries about 'only reading' die hard. You should be prepared to justify USSR, to give details of your proposed programme, useful research evidence and your plans for monitoring and evaluating the work. That will impress. Your other teaching colleagues should also be involved although attempts to organise a whole school programme might be premature at this stage. Like most other school activities USSR works better when supported in a wholehearted way and some teachers will probably wish to take stock of your efforts before committing themselves.

Ancillary staff should also be involved in the discussions as their co-operation is likely to be required when quietness and lack of interruptions are being considered.

Consultation with a number of other adults can also be beneficial. Children's librarians can be extremely helpful, particularly as they can often augment the stock of books available in schools. Contrary to the fears of some teachers, both Advisers and HMIs are likely to be interested. Parents should, of course, have the purpose of USSR made clear to them. Even the acronym needs to be explained. 'I always thought that teacher was a bit of a leftie' was the comment of one parent who perhaps had not received sufficient information.

All visitors to the school should be encouraged to watch USSR at work; preferably they should take part in the activity.

One of the most important groups with whom the activity should be discussed is your class. Members should be told what USSR means and why they are being asked to read silently. They should also be familiar with the necessary procedures, and their suggestions and ideas should be welcomed. Pupil co-operation is strengthened when such discussions take place.

What sort of groups should be involved?

In Primary schools USSR might be organised:

- as a Whole School activity with all the classes taking part at the same time;
- for several classes to work together;
- for a single class;
- for small groups.

It is by no means as difficult to organise Whole School reading in Primary schools as it is in large Secondary establishments where timetabling arrangements are complex. There is something very satisfying about everyone in a school settling down to read on several occasions each week. 'Everyone' is often the operative word for in many schools headteachers, secretaries, class assistants, dinner ladies and caretakers are also involved. Is this going too far? Images of Nero fiddling while Rome burned and Alfred and the cakes keep occurring whenever I read some of the more extreme accounts of USSR. Nor do I take too seriously the apocryphal story of the headteacher who practised USSR outside the school toilets because his example was more likely to be witnessed there than in the relative privacy of his office. Let us be content with adult involvement when it is possible and makes sense.

If Whole School reading is impracticable then several classes practising USSR simultaneously is at least a step in the right direction. If the classrooms are close to one another so much the better, because that will help to ensure that the immediate area is fairly quiet. One of the great strengths of this approach is that it can free teachers for other work. For once USSR is established, close supervision is rarely necessary. Another advantage is that the problem of uncommitted colleagues can be solved by allowing them to do something else.

In most schools USSR is probably practised by individual classes at times which suit them best. These might vary from day to day and week to week. This single class approach is probably the most flexible one.

If other activities in the classroom are not too distracting, there is nothing to stop a small group of pupils being engaged in USSR. Alternatively, when small groups of children are removed from the classroom for remedial work it seems not unreasonable to suggest that some of the time might be devoted to the activity. In addition, when USSR is running smoothly and successfully there seems no reason why individuals should not practise it in their own good time, seeking out a suitable location. This is not as idealistic as it might first appear to be. Indeed, it is probably silent reading in its most natural form. If more of this happened at home then USSR would not be quite so important within the school context. Whether we like it or not, however, responsibility for promoting silent reading rests very much with schools at the present time.

How often should USSR occur?

USSR will only be effective if it takes place with some regularity; once a fortnight would hardly be adequate. Twice a week would seem the absolute minimum. Ideally, it should happen every day. This does not necessarily mean that it should be practised to the point of monotony. Should it seem to be flagging, it can be abandoned for a time. Pupils are then likely to return to it with renewed enthusiasm. Generally, little and often should be the aim.

When should it happen and how long should it last?

There does not seem to be any particular time in the school day which is definitely preferable to another. Reports from a large number of schools indicate that it takes place at the start of the school day, at the end and at every stage between. Timing seems to depend very much upon the organisation of individual schools and classrooms.

Duration is much more clear-cut. It tends to be linked to attention span and thus, to some extent, to age. Very young children are unlikely to read silently for much more than ten minutes however ingenious the organisation, and even this amount of time will have to be worked up to. Older juniors will probably be able to go on for as long as 25 minutes with practice. To go on beyond that might well be counter-productive not only because of loss of concentration but also because there is only so much USSR which school timetables can stand. Exceptionally, some groups of junior children seem to read without much difficulty for well over half an hour at a time.

What can be read?

What should pupils be reading at these times? Dan Fader, an American who popularised the Book Flood approach to reading in schools, recommended teachers to use, within reason, anything which they could lay their hands on. He reported positive results with teenagers when they were supplied with a wide range of materials which included thrillers, specialist publications, newspapers, magazines, paperbacks and comics. Fader's pupils reacted well, read more and seemed to improve in terms of both reading ability and discriminatory powers.

Fader's approach is a powerful one. Everyone requires a range of reading matter. Many adults read fairly widely; few limit themselves to just one level. The same can be said for children. At times they will feel like reading something which is easy and untaxing; on other occasions they will select material more suited to their ability, and occasionally they will be drawn to something which might at first sight appear to be well beyond their powers of concentration. The greater the choice, the better.

There are, of course, reservations. One can have too great a choice. There are only so many books which the normal classroom can cope with. Despite the fact that children will often encounter all sorts of magazines, newspapers and comics at home, some teachers will have reservations about using them during USSR. Decisions must obviously be related to both school policy and commonsense. Personally, I do not think that it is unrealistic to include comics, but I am aware of the doubts which assail many teachers in this respect. I hope to reduce some of these fears in a later chapter.

If a 'books only' policy is adopted then it might well be that school stocks need to be supplemented. Children are usually willing to bring their own books to school and children's librarians can usually be persuaded to assist with block loans. New books should find their way into the collection at regular intervals. This helps to maintain interest. Poetry should be there too and even if comics, newspapers and magazines are absent there must be variety in quality. The mediocre should be mixed with the momentous. Although this book is specifically concerned with children's literature, it would be wrong to imply that USSR should be confined to fiction. Reference books and other sources of information should be there too. Some secondary schools link USSR to particular subjects. Provided that sufficient material can be collected together, it will do no harm if from time to time USSR in the primary school is linked specifically to Science, History, Religious Education or any other subject. Such an approach will go some way towards assisting the much discussed but infrequently implemented concept of 'language across the curriculum'.

Although freedom of choice is vital, some teachers might wish to influence it by grading materials so that their pupils are given some guidance. This might be done by creating 'easy', 'ordinary' and 'hard' sections to the library or by colour coding the books. Care must be taken, however, to ensure that readers understand that such divisions are there to help their choice rather than to confine it.

With children in nursery and reception classes much of the material will be pictorial. Some of the books will have no words in them whatsoever. I see no contradiction in this. Making sense out of pictures is part of the reading process in the early stages. When using such books, young children will believe that they are reading just as they claim that their first scribbles are writing. We should believe them!

Choosing what to read is crucial in one other way: the choice should be made *before* USSR commences. It is impossible to create the right atmosphere when some children are still clustered around the library shelves. Nor does it help if during USSR a constant stream of pupils is going back and forward to change books. Although it might be difficult or even impossible initially, by far the best solution is for every child to have at least two and preferably three pieces of reading material readily available. If what is being read is rejected or completed, then something else can be started without creating a disturbance. This is another good reason for ensuring that there is plenty to read. It is also one of the most important factors in the successful organisation of USSR.

Is silence absolutely necessary?

USSR does not have to be conducted in absolute silence. Very young children do not read in this way in any case. Quietness is probably what most teachers will be looking for. There are, of course, varying degrees of this quality. One should be aiming for something rather different from the hushed reverence of churchgoers or the scholarly whispers to be heard in academic libraries. Teachers will know what I mean when I suggest that there should be a busy quietness in their classrooms when USSR is in progress. Nevertheless, interruptions should be discouraged, particularly those from the variety of messengers who so often visit classrooms.

An important contributory factor in the quest for quietness is comfort. Pupils should be encouraged to spread out. There is no need to be confined to desks. Book corners, easy chairs, cushions and carpets all help to make USSR a relaxed, comfortable activity.

Do teachers read too?

A variety of adults who might be involved has already been mentioned. Most important of all is the supervising teacher, who is usually expected to take part. Some teachers feel uncomfortable about this. They think that they should be marking books, helping children to read or simply supervising the activity in a close, careful way. In fact, once they begin to read their initial reservations are usually lost. Some of them remain at their desks, others read alongside their pupils. Exactly what they read is not important: the latest piece of research in an academic journal, books concerned with professional development, novels, magazines and newspapers have all been recommended. My own preference is a relaxed approach; catching up with children's fiction might be a useful compromise. One teacher with whom I worked created indignation by reading comics. Her pupils felt that she was trespassing.

Inevitably, a teacher's reading will be disturbed from time to time. Young children, particularly, are unlikely to be completely restrained and expressions of enthusiasm or curiosity should not be stifled provided that the ensuing conversations are conducted quietly. Requests for help will also have to be considered and on occasions individual pupils might need to read with the teacher.

Primary pupils are surprisingly perceptive. Many of them will sense that a teacher who is not reading might well be taking a breather. There is nothing dreadfully wrong with that, but children are more likely to be impressed by a teacher who obviously values the activity and takes pleasure in practising it. In short, the teacher should be an effective adult model of behaviour. This is thought by many teachers to be one of the most important factors contributing to the success of USSR.

Does it always work?

Generally, teachers encounter relatively few control problems. Most children enjoy the experience and know that whatever their shortcomings, they are unlikely to be revealed. And as USSR is not followed by mandatory testing it is not a threatening activity. Yet it would be unrealistic to claim that there will never be any problems. The trouble is, you are unlikely to read about them. Reports tend to accentuate the positive.

The most likely reason for failure is that not enough thought has been given to organisation. In such cases a review is obviously necessary. Other failures can occur simply by chance. A disturbance in the playground at break, a sudden flurry of snow or any one of a host of random occurrences can undermine the activity. In such cases it is usually wise to abandon it for something else, preferably an alternative activity such as reading a story. Individual problems, however, are more likely to create disruption than the occasional mass revolution.

The idealistic and oft-reported approach to individual mutineers is to hope that they will be shamed into conformity by the positive response of the great majority of their classmates. If this does not work, there are a number of alternatives. A special effort might be made to provide more suitable material; or for some part of the time a pupil might need to read to the teacher. It might be that the duration of USSR is too lengthy for an individual, in which case other activities should be available for some part of the time. If disruption persists then some positive form of exclusion will have to be considered.

Such possibilities have to be pointed out, but the likelihood of them occurring is small. USSR is, in most cases, a successful, pleasant part of the curriculum.

Is that all there is to it?

For all its popularity USSR will not survive if it becomes too routine. It is sensible to link it to other parts of the language programme. We have already seen in Chapter 3 how literature can be linked to a variety of activities and ideas. Many of them can be used with USSR. A visiting poet, a dramatised story, a relevant videotape or a bookchat, to name but a few examples, can be employed to prevent USSR from flagging.

Children will also react well if their progress is pointed out to them. Comments such as 'Did you realise that you read 14 books last month?' or 'I'm glad that you enjoy cartoon books' will spur children on.

Another important motivator is to encourage children to practise USSR at home. Procedures need to be modified and parents will obviously benefit from advice. Many of them are keen. It is not unusual for them to come into school asking if their absent children can have their USSR reading. Ideally, if such attitudes were universal, USSR would no longer be the responsibility of the school.

How do we know if it is working?

A distinctive feature of most USSR programmes is the insistence that there should not be formal testing. The routine compilation of book reviews or the administration of comprehensive tests would indeed take much of the pleasure away. Nevertheless, some form of evaluation is required. If time is to be allocated to USSR then we have to be able to show that it works.

Teachers' ideas about exactly what it is that they are assessing vary. They usually fall into the following categories:

- reading ability;
- scope of reading;
- attitudes towards reading.

Earlier in this chapter it was claimed that it was highly unlikely that USSR could ever take exclusive credit for the improvement of a pupil's reading ability. Nevertheless, if pupils are reading more frequently than in the past then it is not unreasonable to assume that there might well be some improvement in their reading ability. There is usually no need to test for this reason specifically. Schools test their pupils' reading ability at fairly frequent intervals anyway. Nor is it just overall reading ability which should be considered. Both speed and comprehension might improve. These can be checked by several tests. The Edinburgh Reading Tests are particularly useful in this respect.

Of much greater importance is the monitoring of the scope of pupils' reading. Generally this tends to be neglected in schools. Meticulous records are kept of children's progress in the early stages of learning how to read. Once reasonable competence is achieved records fall away, implying that readers can fend for themselves. Yet how can we really encourage pupils to be interested in books if our knowledge of their reading habits is vague and sketchy? Simple records like those already discussed in Chapter 3 can monitor in an economic way both the quantity and quality of children's reading. They are also likely to be an excellent pointer to the success of USSR.

It has often been claimed that one of the most successful aspects of USSR is the change in attitudes to reading which it helps to create. Teachers can readily devise their own simple questionnaires to determine how enthusiastic their pupils are. The stem approach

> 'I enjoy USSR because . . . . .'
>
> 'I don't like USSR because . . . . .'

is probably a useful starting point. Furthermore, it can pinpoint organisational successes and failures.

With younger children evaluation needs to be verbal. Discussions between the teacher and small groups of pupils is usually effective. For juniors, a particularly good attitude test is already available. Details of Ewing's *Attitudes to Reading* tests can be found in Pumfrey (1985).

Are there other ways by which USSR can be justified?

Where there is doubt about the usefulness of USSR, two methods of persuasion might be used. One of these is to demonstrate a knowledge of relevant investigations and research.

Despite teachers' anxieties about negative attitudes towards sustained reading, it has been frequently advocated for many years. For all his doubts about teachers' motives, mentioned earlier in this chapter, A. J. Jenkinson recognised its worth.

> The potential . . . of these private reading periods is incalculable, for the situation is theoretically one in which education according to its most enlightened tenets should be possible. The pupil is free to choose, in conditions arranged by the teacher. The pupil displays an interest and satisfies an appetite – the teacher influences his self expression and unobtrusively trains his taste. It is an ideal situation.

Concern has not only been for older pupils. Two official documents, *The Handbook of Suggestions for Teachers* (1944) and *Primary Education* (1959) both stressed the need for young pupils to read in quiet and at length. To quote the first mentioned:

> It should on no account be supposed that reading of this kind is something of which only older children are capable.

This plea for more reading time for primary pupils was also taken up in the Plowden Report of 1967.

There is also considerable evidence of the type which might be considered as proof by default. For instance, figures extracted from the somewhat bewildering data in the Bullock Report of 1975 seem to show that 40 per cent of six- and nine-year olds had less than one hour of silent reading of any sort each week.

Further anxieties about the limited range of young children's reading were expressed in two DES surveys in primary education in 1979 and 1982. The report by Lunzer and Gardner of a Schools Council investigation in 1979 underlined these fears. Much reading was discontinuous, fragmented and 'short-burst'. The situation was thought to be less serious in primary schools because of the silent reading done by pupils once other tasks had been completed. This pinpoints one of the great disadvantages of unstructured silent reading: for which pupils are most likely to complete other tasks quickly? It is the bright children who by this arrangement can have more time for silent reading. Slow children might not have any time at all.

In *Extending Beginning Reading*, another Schools Council Report, Southgate provided what was perhaps the most powerful evidence of all. Oral reading in the early years was probably overdone and the amount of time devoted to silent reading, particularly for children of below average ability, was small. Despite their teachers' belief that they preferred reading aloud to adults, three-quarters of a sample of primary pupils stated that they would rather read silently.

It was Vera Southgate who first introduced USSR to a British audience in 1975. Its impact since has been considerable, but it is doubtful if it is being used frequently enough even now. As late as 1988 Gorman, reviewing five years' monitoring of language teaching for the Assessment and Performance Unit, stated that many primary schools did not provide an environment that fostered sustained, exploratory reading.

As already stated, it is difficult to conduct large scale research into the effectiveness of USSR because the approach to it varies from one school to another. Small scale research is just as difficult to find. One recent British investigation, however, provides us with most useful evidence. Wheldall and Entwistle conducted an experiment with third and fourth year juniors in two primary schools. They compared USSR with less structured sessions of silent reading. They discovered that the model which the teacher provided by reading during USSR had a considerable influence on pupils. Once they saw their teachers reading, children settled down to the task much more readily. Moreover, much more actual reading took place in these sessions than in less structured ones. This research might well induce some wry grins. It could be accused of stating the obvious rather like another research, quoted out of context, which was alleged to discover that pupils in comprehensive schools with swimming baths tended to have more swimming lessons than those in comprehensive schools without that facility. It is a pity that careful research if often belittled. Wheldall and Entwistle (1988) have provided evidence which confirms the experiences of many classroom practitioners. Its emphasis of the importance of the teacher's role is particularly valuable. It is an investigation worth quoting.

Cynics cannot have it both ways. If they deride surveys and research, then they can hardly discount descriptions of successful classroom practice in the same breath. This is obviously a second line of persuasion.

USSR has been a popular subject in American journals for many years. Most of the articles, however, are concerned with procedures and evaluation. Accounts of what actually happens in classrooms are sparse. An exception is an account of how USSR can be adapted for very young children. In it Hong describes how she worked with small groups of first year infants of low reading ability. USSR was linked to 'Booktime'. It took place at the same time each day and initially lasted for no more than five minutes. Gradually the time was increased to 15 minutes. The teacher read aloud at the start of each session and her pupils selected from books which had previously been treated in the same way. They could sit anywhere, which made selecting books from the library less disruptive. The teacher read also but was ready to assist with problems and to hear children read. It was permissible to read in pairs and to converse quietly. Children began to respect books. This account is a useful example of how USSR can be adapted creatively to suit the needs of a particular group of children.

Descriptions of practice in the United Kingdom are equally thin on the ground. Maybin, however, reported how Whole School reading was organised in a primary school. Comics were allowed during one session per week and at least two pieces of reading material were pre-selected for all sessions. The activity always occurred immediately after lunch and lasted for 30 minutes, taking place in a relaxed atmosphere. Not every member of staff was convinced that it was effective.

Age range	Name of activity	Time span	Times per week	Number of items used	Comments
Reception Infants	USSR	10 minutes	4	1	Use of a buzzer was popular. One child read with the teacher. Initial chaos due to frequent book changing.
Reception Infants	USLAB	5 minutes, working up to 15 minutes, reverting to 5 minutes at start of a new term.	5	2	Now used throughout the school.
Top Infants	USSR	5 minutes, working up to 15	5	1, 2 later	The teacher experienced difficulty when trying to read herself.
Lower Juniors	USSR	10–20 minutes	3	2	Headteacher had reservations initially.
Third year Juniors	SSR	45 minutes	3	3 or more	The teacher kept a diary of events. Pupils recorded their attitude to SSR.
Third year Juniors	USSR	10–20 minutes	4	4	Pupils' confidence grew as the list of books which they had read increased. There was a measured improvement in reading speed.

(*continues/*)

(continued)

Age range	Name of activity	Time span	Times per week	Number of items used	Comments
Fourth year Juniors	USSR	15–25 minutes	3	4	Children read far more books eventually. Attitudes, as measured by Ewing's ATR tests, generally improved.
Fourth year Juniors	SSR	10–20 minutes	4	3 or more	Headteacher needed much convincing. Activity carefully explained to pupils. Much enthusiasm. Parents called to collect USSR reading for absentees. Pupils' complaints occurred when USSR was not available at school camp.
Moderately slow-learning Juniors in a special school	USSR	5 minutes initially, working up to 15	4	2	Linked to story reading and public library visits. Children valued books for the first time.

A number of teachers with whom I have worked have recorded their experiences. Their comments are summarised in the table.

Clearly, there is no way to organise USSR. Nor is it always successful right from the start. Careful organisation and sensitive modifications usually seem to ensure success eventually.

Sustained reading in the National Curriculum

The National Curriculum does not deal confidently with sustained reading. Its presence is frequently implied but rarely stated. For example, the following is one of several statements which occur in the general introduction to the programme of study for Reading.

> Both boys and girls should experience a wide range of children's literature.

And in the detailed provisions for the same programme it is mentioned on a number of occasions. In section 8, for instance,

> Pupils should read an increasingly wide range and variety of texts in order to become more experienced readers.

There is some indication in section 10 that record-keeping is an important part of the activity. Pupils should:

> ... keep records of their own reading and comment, in writing or in discussion, on the books which they have read.

But only in section 6 is any explicit statement presented: Pupils should '*develop the habit of silent reading*'.

A similar pattern exists throughout the statements of attainment for Reading. There are various hints but only at level 3 does it state that '*Pupils should read silently and with sustained concentration*'.

Does this imply that children cannot be expected to read in a sustained way before level 3? Does it also imply that there is no need to mention it beyond level 3? Uncertainty here is underlined by the fact that this statement of attainment is the only one which is not backed up by any example of how it might be achieved.

Readers of this chapter will, I think, accept that silent reading is appropriate to all children in the primary school be they at level 1 or 5 or anywhere in between. It is simply the organisation and response which will differ from level to level.

By instituting modified forms of silent reading right from the start, teachers will be stealing a march on the National Curriculum. By maintaining reading records of the kind advocated in this chapter they will be able to provide impressive evidence of the scope and volume of their pupils' progress.

It is interesting to note that there are already signs of adjustment in the National Curriculum. In a more recent document (*English – Key Stage 1 – Non-Statutory Guidance*) there is a statement which suggests that teachers need to make provisions for children to engage in sustained, silent reading 'from the earliest age'.

Summary

Sustained reading has an essential part to play in the teaching of children's literature. The responsibility for its promotion rests largely with schools at the present time. It is a fairly modern activity which has sometimes been subjected to neglect and unpopularity.

The best results seem to be achieved when it is planned in a careful way. Rules should be interpreted flexibly but generally the activity should take place in a quiet, comfortable environment in which a wide variety of reading material is available.

Reading matter should be pre-selected and pupils should not be confined to possessing only one publication at once. In this way, disruption is avoided. The teacher's role is extremely important. Children are more likely to take to silent reading if they see that the teacher is taking part in it too.

Although sustained reading should not be formally tested, it is essential to maintain records which show how successful children are in terms of the quantity and versatility of their reading.

Despite the fact that its worth seems obvious, sustained reading of a systematic nature sometimes meets with opposition from teachers. A firm grasp of both theory and practice is likely to dispel most doubts and reservations.

Sustained reading is only part of the language programme but its contribution is considerable. It might well help to improve reading performance.

References

Carsley, J. D. (1957) 'The interest of children (aged 10–11 years) in books'. *British Journal of Educational Psychology* XXVII.

DES (1944) *Handbook of suggestions for Teachers*. HMSO.

DES (1959) *Primary Education*. HMSO.

DES (1978) *Primary Education in England and Wales*. HMSO.

DES (1982) *Education 5 to 9*. HMSO.

Fader, D. (1969) *Hooked on Books*. Pergamon Press.

Fenwick, G. (1988) *Uninterrupted, Sustained, Silent Reading*. Reading and Language Information Centre, University of Reading.

Fox, G. (1978) 'Thereby hangs a tale'. *Times Educational Supplement*, 11.7.78.

Gorman, T. *et al.* (1988) *Language Performance in Schools*. HMSO.

Hong, L.K. (1981) 'Modifying SSR for Beginning Readers'. *The Reading Teacher*, May.

Jenkinson, A.J. (1940) *What do Boys and Girls Read?* Methuen and Co.

Lee, Laurie (1975) *I Can't Stay Long*. Andre Deutsch.

Lunzer, E. and Gardner, K. (1979) *The Effective Use of Reading*. Heinemann.

Maybin, J. (1983) 'Whole School Reading Periods' in Hoffman *et al.*, *Children, Language and Literature*. Open University Press.

Southgate, V. (1981) *Extending Beginning Reading*. Heinemann.

Wheldall, K. and Entwistle, J. (1988) 'Back in the USSR.' *Educational Psychology* Vol. 8, nos. 1&2.

Other useful reading

(*The Reading Teacher* and *Journal of Reading* are published in USA but are available at most University, Polytechnic and College of HE libraries in this country.)

Gambrell, L.B. (1978) 'Getting started with SSR and keeping it going'. *The Reading Teacher*, December.

Ganz, P. and Theofield, M.B. (1974) 'Suggestions for starting SSR'. *The Journal of Reading*, May.

Heathington, B.S. (1979) 'What to do about Reading Motivation in the Middle School'. *Journal of Reading*, May.

Hunt, L. (1970) 'The effect of self selection, interest and motivation upon instructional and frustrational levels'. *The Reading Teacher*, Vol. 4, No. 2.

Kaisen, J. (1987) 'SSR/Booktime: Kindergarten and first grade Sustained Silent Reading'. *The Reading Teacher*, February.

McCracken, R.A. (1971) 'Initiating Sustained Silent Reading'. *Journal of Reading*, May.

Moore, J.C. *et al.* (1980) 'What we know after a decade of Sustained Silent Reading'. *The Reading Teacher*, January.

Mork, T.A. (1972) 'SSR in the classroom'. *The Reading Teacher*, February.

Pumfrey, P.D. (1985) *Reading Tests and Assessment Techniques* (2nd ed). Hodder and Stoughton. (Includes details of Edinburgh Reading Tests and Ewing's ATR.)

Sadoski, M.C. (1980) 'An attitude survey for Sustained Silent Reading Programs'. *Journal of Reading*, May.

CHAPTER 5

Poetry Counts

The state of poetry

Had this chapter been written five years ago it would have been very different. At that time the cloud of gloom which had for many years been hanging over poetry in schools showed few signs of dispersing. It would be both depressing and pointless to discuss the many surveys and official documents which have written poetry off, but the overall picture created is one of most children disliking poetry and the lessons associated with it.

Far from encouraging children to like poetry, schools seemed to do just the opposite. To quote Terry, the principal character in the film *The Likely Lads*: 'I don't like poetry. I was put off it at an early age.' Terry was probably echoing the sentiments of James Bolam, the actor who played the part, and many other people too. Even in the early 1980s official documents were still writing poetry off as a bad job.

Circumstances have changed – although hinting at this in an article written in 1986 I was subjected to some severe criticism. Nevertheless, poetry in school is certainly much more buoyant now than it has ever been.

What was wrong with poetry? What is right about it now? To find some answers it might be useful to start with what happened when many of today's teachers were pupils.

Nursery rhymes at home and school were often a good start. They might be followed by poems read by the teacher to the whole class, each pupil having a copy of the identical anthology. This might be the only poetry book available in the classroom. The teacher would ask questions at the end of the reading; often the teacher would supply most of the answers. Then there was the copying down of poems which had to be learned. A good combination this; writing practice and memorisation. But the poems were rarely the pupils' choice.

Did the children write many poems? I wrote one about Robin Hood when I was eight. But I did this at home. In eleven years of schooling no one ever asked me to write a poem. Some adults might have had a different experience from this but mine seems fairly typical.

If anything, I fared worse at Grammar school. There were some patriotic poems, fashionable at the time, in the first two years. I borrowed the *Rubaiyat* from the school library and the English teacher thought I wanted it for the erotic pictures. Later there was an examination of poetic structure: then nothing. During all that time I memorised two poems: 'The Eagle' by Tennyson and 'The End of Days' by Walter Raleigh. No one asked me to do this, I did it because I liked the poems. After that, I forgot about poetry for a long time.

My re-kindled interest coincided with the start of my teaching career. At first I read the slim volumes of up and coming poets like Jon Silkin, Ted Hughes, Thomas Gunn and Philip Larkin and gradually I began to look for children's poetry. I discovered that primary children liked having poems read to them, provided that they did not have to answer too many questions afterwards. I discovered that they actually liked to write poetry. I can still remember fragments of it to this day, as well as the name of writers.

Here Philip, aged nine, describes his journey across the snow-deadened desolation of the playground on his way to the outside toilet:

In the playground, it is snowing,
There is no one to see,
The wind is hardly blowing,
There is no one but me.

Pat, aged ten, writes of playtime activities towards the end of the Easter term:

At half past ten
The bell will ring,
Ding-a-ling, ding-a-ling,
Ding-a-ling-ding.
Look around and you will see
Boys in rugby colours of a bee.
Soon the bell will ring again,
Ding-a-ling-ding-a-ling.
Ding-a-ling, ding.

And Peter, aged eight, combines an actual experience and a fertile imagination:

As I was walking down Vicar Lane,
I heard somebody cry,
Oh help me, Oh help me,
Oh help me, Oh do,
Somebody has knocked me over,
Whatever should I do?
When I picked him up
I found he was only two.
I said, 'Whoever could of done this to you?'
He said, 'It was my pa, he is a bad man,
He knocked me over with his motor van.'

Yet despite the enthusiasm which pupils displayed for poetry, it was hard to keep teaching it. One headteacher whom I respected both as a person and an educator remarked to me: 'You like poetry, don't you!' It was as though he had identified a perversion.

Too few poetry books, too much analysis, a minority subject treated with suspicion, that was what was wrong. And today? More poetry books than ever before, a wealth of new approaches, and a rather more enlightened public image. It was not before time.

During the last decade poetry has become more widely popular. Poetry competitions attract large entries. And poetry is losing its snobbishness. Many people are now familiar with the works of Philip Larkin, Ted Hughes and Seamus Heaney, probably because of the increased media exposure which they have been given. Many others will be familiar with the poetry of Roger McGough, Brian Patten, Lynton Kwesi Johnson and John Cooper Clarke. Even more people probably know Pam Ayres. In this way poetry might be compared to music. While most of us acknowledge that some types of music might be better than others, this is to some extent a matter of taste. We acknowledge and usually tolerate the existence of all kinds of music. That is how it should be with poetry.

Many influential teachers have been attracted by the ideas of the educator and anthologist, Michael Benton. In two immensely useful articles published in 1978 he raised a number of important issues including:

- Is there really a dearth of poetry for children, or can its negative image be attributed to unimaginative teaching?
- Do teachers read poetry?
- Why is poetry treated separately, as though it was on the

periphery of children's literature rather than being an integral part of it?

If report after report claims that poetry is unpopular without providing any suggestions about how this situation might be changed, is it any wonder that it has been in the doldrums? Fortunately, many teachers have taken up Michael Benton's challenge.

Another useful influence has been the article '36 Things to do with a poem' by Geoff Fox and Brian Merrick. This has appeared in a number of publications. The authors admit that the activities which it suggests are by no means original. Nevertheless, for many teachers it will provide new ways of approaching poetry.

Then there is the work of Sandy Brownjohn. Her three small books published in the 1980s have had a profound influence upon the way children and teachers approach poetry writing.

These, then, may be regarded as the major influences in the gradual improvement of poetry teaching. Another looms on the horizon. The National Curriculum requires primary school pupils to listen and respond to poetry, to write it and, perhaps more controversially, to learn it by heart.

The use of poetry

The deep-seated unease which poetry in schools has attracted until fairly recently means that its justification is essential. It is hoped that the following points will go at least some way towards achieving this.

(1) Poetry is an important part of the literary heritage of this and other lands. (Our best known writer, William Shakespeare, made extensive use of poetic language.)
(2) It makes use of language in imaginative, sensitive and emotional ways.
(3) Its relative brevity makes it ideal for conveying incidents, events and reflections which would be difficult to express in prose.
(4) It possesses a wide variety of structures.
(5) It encourages precision in speech and writing.
(6) It encourages experimentation in speech and writing.
(7) Properly presented, it is a pleasurable experience.
(8) Its rhymes and alliteration are powerful factors in the development of children's ability to spell and read.

Beyond what might be termed 'deficit' research, investigations concerned with poetry are few. By deficit research I mean the many surveys which indicate that poetry is unpopular and poorly presented. A gleam of light can be identified in a number of papers written by Lynette Bradley. Longitudinal studies which included intensive practice revealed that both rhyme and alliteration markedly assisted children's spelling and reading. There are implications here for both home and school.

Finding out about poetry

Because poetry has been neglected it is not surprising that information about it can be difficult to obtain. The stock of school and class libraries can be checked and colleagues consulted, but it is likely that more information will be obtained from children's librarians. The amount of poetry in public libraries is often surprisingly high.

Publishers' catalogues are much more useful than they used to be because as interest in poetry increases so does the number of books available. There are now probably more poetry books for children being published than ever before.

The London based Book Trust, formerly known as the National Book League, offers a travelling collection of poetry books for a price which a school or a group of schools will find affordable. The present collection is a little out of date, but that is likely to be rectified shortly.

The poetry boom has coincided with the publication of one of the best books about children's poetry ever to be produced. Styles and Triggs's *Poetry 0–16* is brimming with details of nursery rhymes, poetry picture books, word plays, anthologies, comic verse, limericks, ballads and much more for various age groups. It also contains interesting comments on poets past and present. This magnificent books deserves to be up-dated and republished every five years. Another useful source is *101 Good Poetry Books* by Anne Rowe.

Which poetry? Which poets?

There seems to have been no investigation of children's reading interests and preferences which deals exclusively with poetry. So prediction about what is liked and acceptable must be tentative even though based on common sense and experience.

Very young children enjoy poetry with a pronounced rhythm. They like repetition and alliteration. Hence nursery rhymes, playground rhymes and finger-plays are all popular. The strong rhythm of most of

A. A. Milne's poetry probably explains why he remains so popular despite the dated nature of some of his material.

Both infants and juniors like humour as long as it is not too subtle. Humorous verse might be sub-divided into nonsense and comic poetry. Both have strong traditions in our language. Those masters of nonsense verse, Edward Lear and Lewis Carroll, are still popular and the tradition is kept alive by such contemporary poets as Spike Milligan and Roger McGough. As for writers of comic verse, you might start with Hilaire Belloc and work your way through Ogden Nash, Shel Siverstein, Kit Wright, Mike Rosen, and Alan Ahlberg. It is worth remembering that even the funniest poets have, like clowns, a serious side to their work. Anyone who has read Kit Wright's 'Useful Person' or the haunting 'First Day at School' by Roger McGough will vouch for that.

Primary school children of all ages usually like poems with a story. They will find them in collections of ballads and narrative poems, though exactly what constitutes a story-poem is difficult to define. Consequently, examples can also be found in anthologies and collections by individual poets.

Poetry books for younger pupils

The Great Big Book of Nursery Rhymes (Peggy Blakeley)
The Mother Goose Treasury (Iona and Peter Opie)
The Puffin Book of Nursery Rhymes
Roger was a Razor Fish (Jill Bennett)

Poetry books for older primary pupils

Peacock Pie (Walter de la Mare)
Complete Poems for Children (James Reeves)
Wouldn't you like to know? (MIchael Rosen)
Figgle Hobbin (Charles Causley)

Poets for younger primary pupils

Quentin Blake
Allen Ahlberg
A. A. Milne
Edward Lear
Robert Louis Stevenson
Stanley Cook
Shirley Hughes

Poets for older primary pupils

Edward Lear
Lewis Carroll
Roger McGough
Eleanor Farjeon
James Reeves
Kit Wright
Ted Hughes
Charles Causley

As they grow older, Primary pupils begin to appreciate reflective poems, nature poetry and even poems which deal with fairly insignificant incidents and events. Some of these poems will be serious.

This is a good thing. If there is a weakness in the present poetry boom it is an over emphasis on the comic and amusing. Coupled with this there is often too much stress on rhyming which results in poetry deteriorating into rather ordinary verse. Serious poetry, provided it is not pompous, seems to avoid these pitfalls.

Teachers are urged to search out anthologies and collections which they themselves enjoy for these are most likely to work for them. For those who feel they need a starting point, some suitable books and authors are suggested in the table on the previous page.

Many poets writing mainly for an adult audience have produced some poems which have found favour with children. Robert Browning's 'Pied Piper of Hamelin' and Christina Rosetti's 'Goblin Market' are outstanding examples. Other poets might write a great deal for young people, yet with the exception of one or two poems, their work is forgotten. Many readers might recognise the following lines:

> 'Twas the night before Christmas, when all through the house
> Not a creature was stirring, not even a mouse . . .

Some might even identify the poem as 'A Visit from St Nicholas' and the poet as Clement Moore. But very few will be familiar with any other poems by this American writer.

Poets who have written with consistent success for young audiences and whose work has endured in quantity are by no means frequent. Virtually all of them, with the exception of Hilaire Belloc, are represented in the table.

Reading poetry

This section is not about reading aloud, either by teacher or pupil. It is about poetry being read silently. If this has not happened frequently enough in the past it is probably because sufficient poetry was not available. It follows, therefore, that there has to be a good supply of anthologies and the works of individual poets in both school and class libraries. Ideally, poetry and prose should not be separated on the library shelves because the division is rather artificial and tends to work against poetry. But if reading poetry has only occurred infrequently or not at all, then it might be advisable to place all the poetry books together. In the type of silent reading session which has been outlined in Chapter 4, poetry will probably be read from time to time without any pressure being exerted on pupils. But more than this might be needed if there is little tradition of poetry reading in class.

The answer might be to reserve some silent reading sessions for poetry only. More realistically, it might be encouraged by lessons in which children, having been given some warning, discuss favourite poems and poets. No doubt some of the activities described in the following section will also assist.

Whatever the strategy, it is important that children should read poetry frequently. For both children and adults poetry might be compared to crosswords or jig-saw puzzles. Familiarity usually improves understanding of the task involved. The best way to become familiar with poetry is to read it.

Working with poetry

This section reviews the many activities, other than writing, which can be associated with poetry. It begins with three of my own ideas. They are unlikely to be original, but at the time when they were tried out, I was unaware of similar work going on elsewhere.

1. Know a poet

Is it possible that at times we concentrate too much on poetry and too little on the people who write it? Children are naturally interested in other human beings and the majority of poets are interesting people.

- Robert Burns traced poems, usually abusive ones, in the dust on carriage doors.
- John Clare wrote some of his best poetry when incarcerated in Northampton Asylum.
- Philip Larkin once attended a reading of his poetry in disguise.

Admittedly, Larkin's poems are not relevant to primary school pupils, but they serve to illustrate a point.

Some years ago a pupil studying for O-level English Literature came to me with a request for help with 'Toads', one of Larkin's shorter poems. I helped him solve his problems as best I could and received a message from his English teacher. 'How do you know all this?' My reply was simple. I have been interested in Larkin for 30 years and knowing a lot about him had helped me to understand his poetry.

Children admire expertise in most fields. If you know about poets and demonstrate this, some of your pupils will want to do the same. This makes poetry more intersting.

The nature poet John Clare also fascinates me. Many of his poems can be used at primary level. He is buried in the village of Helpston, and the Middle School there is named after him. I hope to go there soon.

Children can adopt their own poets in this way. Quite apart from anything else, it will help to de-mystify the profession. Asking children about poets often produces stereotypes like the following:

. . . wears glasses
. . . looks brainy
. . . has a beard
. . . wears a cloak
. . . is posh
. . . has plenty of money.

A rich poet? There are not many of them about! By studying poets children will recognise that you cannot pin them down in this way. And they will probably come to understand poetry better. Know poets – know poetry!

2. *Spoken poetry*

It's extremely satisfying to learn a poem if you really want to. If not, it can be excruciating. You are much more likely to make your pupils enthusiastic about memorisation if you can do it yourself.

At present I am learning 'Flannan Isle', an exciting and powerful poem by a fellow Northumbrian, Wilfred Gibson. Hitherto I have read it with success to older juniors. Without a book the poem's impact will be greater. My present repertoire consists of some 15 poems, mostly for secondary pupils. I hope to expand it.

Memorising poetry takes time. It is less easy than learning a story. In my experience it has to be built up bit by bit.

To encourage children to memorise poems a reasonably free choice of material has to be allowed. In the case of lengthy poems extracts might be selected, or a number of pupils might pool their resources, each taking a part. Once the learning has been reasonably accomplished then its presentation should be polished up, making use of the same verbal skills which are used in story telling. Delivery has to be lively. There is nothing worse than a sing-song recitation.

While readily acknowledging the excellence of polished public performance, my own view is that organised choral speaking is too formal an exercise for the primary classroom. Nevertheless, provided it is not overdone, the basic idea of dramatising and acting out poems is a good one, especially if there is an element of dialogue. The traditional poem 'Widdecombe Fair' is a good example in this respect.

Spoken poetry (recitation sounds too formal) is popular with very young children. This is probably because they are extremely sensitive to rhythm. The writer Karen Blixen once aptly described rhythm as 'speaking like rain'. Rain soaking into long-dry earth? Rain drumming on the roof tops? Rain crashing down in torrents? It does not matter. One of the most useful experiences which teachers can given to young children is to help them speak 'like rain'. The rain will fall not only – Butch Cassidy-like – onto their heads but also into them.

There are a number of ways to make spoken poetry attractive. Some are suggested in the table.

Short poems	These are often amusing. They do not take long to learn.
Tongue twisters	Based on alliteration. Learning them appeals to many children's competitive instinct.
Cumulative poems	Here the poem is built up gradually with only one or two new lines being added with each verse. 'The House that Jack Built' is a good example. The sheer repetition helps many children to learn such poems without really trying.
Counting poems	Ten Green Bottles, for example. Young children enjoy counting rhymes, acting them out with hands and fingers.
Action rhymes	Young children enjoy indicating what is happening in these poems.
Story poems	Can be dramatised.
Rhythmic poems	When rhythm is strong, the learning of poetry becomes more easy.
Poems with a chorus	Everyone joins in and the chorus, at least, is quickly learned.
Songs	Poetry to music – and easily learned.
Repetitions	Some poems have a common start to each verse – like Allan Ahlberg's 'Please Mr Butler'. Others, like 'The Daniel Jazz' by N. Vachel Lindsay, have many repetitive lines. In such circumstances, learning is not difficult.
Children's own poems	Usually fairly short. There is a great deal of incentive to learn a poem of your own creation.
Playground games and jingles	Many children know some of these already and will happily research others.
Football chants	Once again, many of these are known already.
Poems for two voices	In some poems there are two clear speaking parts.
Collaborative verse	A poem can be divided up for a number of voices and, perhaps, a chorus too.

Poetry for learning can be funny, serious, frightening or reflective. Ideally, the language should be vigorous. Above all, it has to interest the individual who is learning it.

3. *Visit a poem*

Mention of Widdecombe Fair reminds me that there is, in fact, a fair in that Dartmoor village in early September. On the village green ponies graze around a monument on which the poem is carved.

In the Cheshire village of Daresbury, the church has a large stained-glass window commemorating Lewis Carroll's *Alice in Wonderland*. Carroll was born in the village, where his father was the Vicar. Not far from the church, the local primary school has an Alice in Wonderland weather vane. Lewis Carroll wrote almost 200 books, most of them scholarly works. Best known for Alice, he was also a talented writer of nonsense verse, such as 'The Walrus and the Carpenter' and 'Jabberwocky.'

Knowsley Hall, near Prescot in Lancashire, is now well known for its Safari Park. In Victorian times the Earl of Derby maintained a menagerie there. He employed a talented painter to record his impressions of the birds and animals. Fond of children, the painter made up poems for the Earl's children in his spare time. His name was Edward Lear. In 1988 pupils from Knowsley LEA compiled a book of limericks to celebrate the poet's link with their locality.

Of course, not everyone is lucky enough to be close to the origins of poets and poems, although it is surprising what a little research can unearth. Visits to these places can do much to create an increased interest in poetry.

4. *Small group discussion*

Most of my ideas about small group discussion have been obtained from the writings of David and Elizabeth Grugeon and Michael Benton. It is an approach I have used frequently and encourage students and teachers to do likewise. Its main advantage is that it gives pupils time to think and talk in ways which are not possible in the conventional class lesson. Poetry is ideally suited to small group discussion because it is a condensed form of literature; a poem can usually be discussed in its entirety within the space of one session.

Setting up opportunities for small group discussion requires careful planning. The following points need to be considered.

- Ten minutes is probably the optimum amount of time needed for primary pupils. With experience older pupils might be able to extend this to 15 minutes; younger children might require no more than five minutes.
- Groups should be fairly small. Five is ideal, three is too small and more than six is unwieldy. Four or five usually guarantees a good variety of opinion without squeezing out shy or less articulate children.
- Each member of the group should have a copy of the poem.
- Merely asking the group to discuss the poem is usually quite sufficient. Too specific a brief usually inhibits participants and deprives them of initiative. If more guidance is required, the following transcript will indicate what factors children seem to take into account when they attempt this type of work.
- Small group discussion should not be overdone. Bearing in mind that it will probably be used in other areas of the curriculum, once every fortnight should be sufficient.
- It should not be used in isolation. It is only part of the poetry programme.
- The results of discussions should be reported. Without this the work can lack purpose.

The transcript is of a discussion of 'The Apple Raid' by Vernon Scannell. The poem, though short, is rather more complicated than it might appear at first glance. The subject is usually attractive to older juniors, perhaps appealing to their primitive hunting instincts. The five fourth-year junior boys attend a school where there is no great tradition of poetry teaching. Nor is poetry likely to be found in their homes. Yet their work is lively, enthusiastic and perceptive.

The Apple Raid

Darkness came early, though not yet cold;
Stars were strung on the telegraph wires;
Street lamps spilled pools of liquid gold;
The breeze was spiced with garden fires.

That smell of burnt leaves, the early dark,
Can still excite me but not as it did
So long ago when we met in the park —
Myself, John Peters and David Kidd.

We moved out of town to the district where
The lucky and wealthy had their homes
With garages, gardens, and apples to spare
Ripely clustered in the trees' green domes.

We chose the place we meant to plunder
And climbed the wall and dropped down to
The secret dark. Apples crunched under
Our feet as we moved through the grass and dew.

The clusters on the lower boughs of the tree
Were easy to reach. We stored the fruit
In pockets and jerseys until all three
Boys were heavy with their tasty loot.

Safe on the other side of the wall
We moved back to town and munched as we
went.
I wonder if David remembers at all
That little adventure, the apples' fresh scent?

Strange to think that he's fifty years old,
That tough little boy with scabs on his knees;
Stranger to think that John Peters lies cold
In an orchard in France beneath apple trees.

Vernon Scannell

MICHAEL It's a good story.
PETER I like that bit where they get over the wall.
DANNY I think they left because the fellah was coming, yeah. I like it though.
MICHAEL They went to get fruit in a park.
JOHN It's not a park, it's a back yard.
MICHAEL It was a back yard, they climbed the wall, somebody chased them and they went back to the city.
PETER It might be like that. I like that bit 'The breeze was spiced with garden fires'. It just sounds good.
GERARD I like the part 'Street lamps spilled pools of liquid gold'. It's just the light shining circles on the pavement. I've seen them.
DANNY It's great that, yeah, especially the orange ones. I like that.
JOHN There's the part when he's thinking back to when he had scabs on his knees.
PETER Or the part where they get over the wall and all the apples are crunching.
ALL Yeah.
DANNY [*Makes crunching sound. All giggle*.]
MICHAEL Who's this fellah John Peters beneath apple trees?
JOHN [*Ignoring this*] It makes you feel as if you're there.
PETER He's dead in France.
GERARD It's a sad ending where his mate died.
MICHAEL It must be sixty years old then.
DANNY Someone did that on the radio where he went into the future.
MICHAEL He was stealing 'cos they didn't have any money. They had the rations then.
DANNY Oh, yeah.
PETER This was probably World War Two.
JOHN 1930 odd, I reckon.

DANNY Maybe they robbed the apples 'cos they didn't have the money.
GERARD They just done it for fun.
[*Brief discussion all joining in, about apples and stealing from local trees, being chased etc.*]
MICHAEL The name's good 'The Apple Raid'.
DANNY It sounds like a bank raid.
[*Laughter all round.*]
GERARD It sounds like the tree's a bank and a squirrel is a bank manager.
DANNY Yeah, guarding the nuts.
[*More laughter. Some jumbled discussion about seeing in the dark and so forth. Most people talking over others.*]
MICHAEL It must be autumn with them burning leaves and apples falling and that.
GERARD Yeah, the lights were on and 'Darkness came early'.
MICHAEL All that time past in a little poem.
PETER Fifty years on one, two, three, four, five, six, seven paragraphs.
DANNY It must have been about 1935.
JOHN Yes, but you've got to consider when he wrote it though, haven't you.
[*Pause.*]
MICHAEL 'He lies cold in an orchard in France'. He must have got killed.
DANNY The Second World War.
JOHN Yes, in France.
DANNY They weren't fighting in France, were they?
GERARD No, but they were over there helping them.
PETER Oh yeah, because the Germans were invading them.
DANNY It says dew, it must have been raining.
JOHN Dew isn't rain, it's early in the morning, like moisture on the grass.
[*Much joint discussion about the height of the wall and the possibility of it being Lord Derby's.*]
PETER I still like that bit about 'tasty loot', it makes me hungry.
GERARD The top's the best: 'Stars were strung on the telegraph wires'. The stars were in the sky right, and they look like they were hanging there.
[*More joint discussion about stealing from apple trees and retrieving lost balls from neighbours' gardens. Much bravado from Danny.*]
MICHAEL I used to think that long poems were boring, but this one was good.
DANNY I like it 'cos it's time going back from his memory.
PETER It isn't true though.
JOHN Of course, it's true. He mentions their names' look how that lad has grown up now. Look . . . 'Strange to think he's fifty year old'. You know he had scabs on his knees and he's still alive.
DANNY Birchy, which bit do you like?
MICHAEL I like the bit at the beginning.
PETER I like where he's looking back.
DANNY 'That smell of burnt leaves, the early dark can still excite me'. Oh, he must have gone back and didn't enjoy it as much.
JOHN No. I know what he meant by that. The smell of the leaves now reminds him of when he was little.
DANNY Oh. Maybe.

What are the members of this group doing when they discuss this poem?

- They are appreciating the poet's use of words and phrases. (This poem attracts comment which is almost wholly positive. Negative comments should not be discouraged if, in the opinion of group members, they are deserved.)
- They relate sections of the poem to their own experience.
- They work out the meanings of words, phrases and sentences.
- They are estimating the overall value of the poem.

Some of this is quite complicated. Note the prolonged discussion about the poem's time scale. Try working this out for yourself. It is by no means easy.

It is possible to look at the transcript in another way.

- All five pupils contribute to the discussion.
- One, Michael, seems to lead the discussion and ensures its continuity.
- Two, John and Gerard, do not seem to participate as frequently as the others.
- Agreement, disagreement, modification and reasoning are all in evidence.

Could these pupils have obtained as much from a class discussion? The answer must be a resounding 'No'. There would simply not have been enough time for them to talk out their ideas and they would have been dependent on the teacher's lead. Communication would have been mainly one way. That is not to say that small group discussion diminishes the teacher's role, it simply changes it. As already stated this sort of discussion must not be an isolated experience. It should take place within a context which allows for the exchange of opinions in a variety of ways. The following structure seems to be appropriate.

(1) The teacher reads the poem to the whole class and asks for comments.
(2) The teacher reads the poem again, probably with more emphasis.
(3) The pupils move into pre-arranged groups and begin to discuss the poem.
(4) The teacher might move from group to group, particularly if the children are inexperienced: otherwise they might be left to get on with it. Teacher intervention should rarely occur, perhaps only if requested.
(5) Some of the discussions, at least, should be taped.

(6) Once there are signs that most of the groups are moving towards a conclusion, the class should re-assemble.
(7) The teacher will ask for the opinions of each group, modifying them where necessary.
(8) The teacher will summarise the work in terms of effectiveness and what has been discovered.

The difference between class discussion and small group work might be illustrated (see Figure 5.1). The second approach generates far more ideas and opinions. Furthermore, it helps children to realise that teachers do not hold a monopoly in terms of literary knowledge.

Figure 5.1 The difference between class discussion and small group discussion

Class discussion

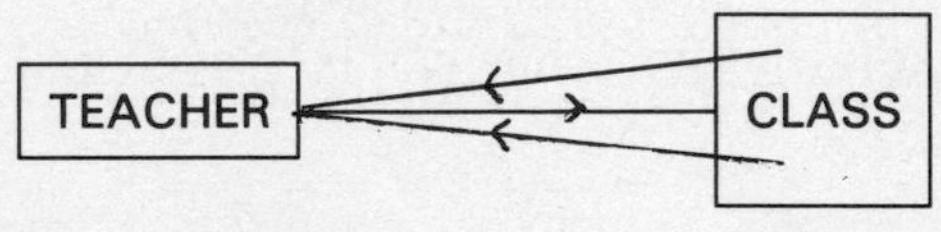

Small group discussion in context

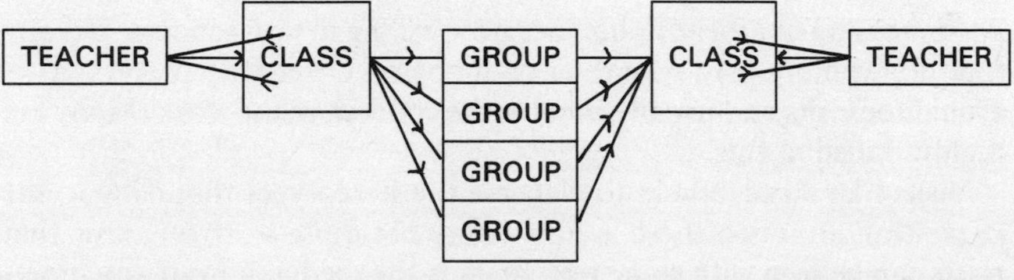

The most difficult part of this work is the use of transcripts. It is asking far too much to make use of them all. Merely listening to one from each group in an average sized class would take at least an hour. One has to be selective. After all, play-back is simply a means of checking if all is going well. Since a general impression can usually be gained from the whole class discussion which should round off these sessions, play-back need be used only sparingly. It can be used with much more frequency by pupils who will find listening to their recorded deliberations useful prior to reporting back to the class as a whole.

Transcript analysis is even more time-consuming but it is worth the effort, even if it is just once a term, to check over a tape. The results are invariably illuminating and in most cases very rewarding. Although there is the occasional failure, most teachers with whom I have worked have been surprised and delighted at the quality of the discussion. In the words of one experienced teacher: 'Just to get them talking about poetry is really something.'

Group discussion improves with practice. In its early stages it tends to be rather short and participants flit from one issue to the next with little evidence of resolution. After several sessions the discussion is usually lengthier and more positive, with solutions being attempted before another point is raised.

As we saw in chapter three, how children respond will depend to some extent upon age and level of maturity. Every member of a group should be able to read the poem being discussed without too much difficulty. This implies that many very young children will have to be excluded from this kind of work. That might be so but it is not difficult to devise a similar experience using taped poems. Provided these are at the right level and fairly short they can be played and replayed during brief discussions.

5. *Visiting poets*

An increasing number of poets are now willing to visit schools. Usually they do far more than read their own poetry. Often they prefer two or even three visits and usually involve the children in the work. Many are highly skilled at this.

Visits like this can help to disperse the stereotypes that cling to the profession although these are probably not quite so strong now that poets can be seen with some regularity in the media. Few, if any, poets are sufficiently well paid to give their services for nothing but Regional Art Councils can be quite generous with their help to schools in this respect.

6. *Poetry festivals*

These can last a half-day, a day or even go on for a week. They can be based in one school or several. Ideally they should involve visiting poets. The programme should be varied both in activities and audience size and might include:

- Themes – for example, poetry of town and country.
- Story poems – 'The Pied Piper of Hamelin' is a good example.
- Poetry in song – nursery rhymes, advertising jingles, traditional songs, popular ballads.
- Writing workshops – write a limerick, concoct a couplet.

- Poet of the year award – for various age groups.
- Dramatised versions – try 'The Quangle Wangle's Hat' by Edward Lear.
- Displays of poetry books – booksellers, publishers or the Book Trust will probably oblige.
- Class anthologies – typed or word processed and illustrated by children, these can be very attractive.
- A riddle or tongue twister competition – obviously, the best approach for young children will be an oral one.
- A cumulative poem – each pupil to provide a line.
- A performance of action rhymes.
- Spoken poetry by both pupils and teachers.

7. *Poetry in public*

British Rail have for some time displayed a series of poster poems in the London Underground. The scheme involves the work of well known poets and is directed at an adult audience. Such a welcome attempt to popularise poetry might be extended in at least two ways.

It might be possible, for instance, to persuade local transport firms, department stores, even garages, to display the printed work of well known poets, local or otherwise. Some of this poetry should be intended for children. It would be amusing to see buses travelling about Merseyside carrying some of Roger McGough's 'P.C. Plod' poems on their sides.

Might this wider audience also be available to young poets? Almost two decades ago, the Priority Education movement persuaded local shopkeepers to display children's work in their windows. Children's librarians are often keen to do this too. Local newspapers, stations, police stations, hospitals, even car stickers might be put to use in a similar way. Children's work is often fresh and unspoilt. Displayed in this way it would bring pleasure to many people in environments not always noted for their brightness. It would also bring pride and a sense of achievement to the originators and their families. My two young friends Andrew and Daniel would provide excellent copy.

A butterfly
who swallowed
an elephant
did not burp,
instead
he said,
'Belly-bent'.

(*Andrew, aged 8*)

Slowly
Very slowly
Tortoise creeps along
Its hard shell is very break-proof
armour

(*Daniel, aged 10*)

8. Other ideas

There are many approaches to poetry. You will find a great number in the book *Children, Language and Literature*, among them Fox and Merrick's celbrated '36 Things to do with a Poem'. Others can be found in Calthrop and Ede's *Not 'Daffodils' again*, which is distinctly classroom based. Teachers can consult these and other sources listed at the end of this chapter. They should not be overwhelmed with the mass of ideas but adapt them to their own needs. Equally important, they should try to devise some of their own. There is always room for new ideas.

The following ideas culled from the sources mentioned above particularly attract me.

- Poetry sharing: Teachers and children discuss poems which they have discovered.
- Instant reaction: Children write or draw their impressions of a poem during or immediately after it has been read to them.
- Different versions: Individuals or groups read a poem in different ways – quickly, quietly, loudly, dramatically.
- Poetry tapes: Poets and skilled readers on cassettes can be listened to individually or in groups.

9. 36 things not to do with a poem

Chapter 3 mentioned the danger of over-kill. I have similar reservations about the great flurry of activity which carries poetry along these days. Welcome as it is, we need to be sure that poetry is not swept away by it. Children need time to read poetry and at times will prefer to do that unfettered by associated activities. Even after a poem has been read to a class, there are times when there needs to be no probing whatsoever. Many powerful poems speak for themselves. Take, for example, 'Mid-Term Break' by Seamus Heaney, a short poem which builds up tension line by line, revealing its last secret only in the final five words. Its impact is immense. The vast majority of children over eight will recognise this and understand the poem. That is where it should be left.

Poetry and the National Curriculum

A very positive approach is taken here. There is a wealth of suggestions, both for Reading and for Speaking and Listening. Ideas about writing poetry seem to be more limited and are dealt with, in any case, in the chapter which follows this one.

Both programmes of study and statements of attainment abound with ideas. It is pleasing to see poetry treated in this way. Some examples are given below.

> ... listening and responding to stories, rhymes, poems and songs (*Programme of Study for Speaking and Listening – detailed provisions for key stage 1*).
>
> ... telling stories, and reciting poems which have been learnt by heart (*Programme of Study for Speaking and Listening – detailed provisions for key stage 1*).
>
> ... listen and respond to an increasing range of poetry and plays (*Programme of Study for Speaking and Listening – general provisions for key stages 2 to 4*).
>
> ... talking about stories and poems (*Programme of Study for Speaking and Listening – general provisions for key stages 2 to 4*).
>
> ... listen attentively, and respond to stories and poems (*Statement of Attainment, level 1 – Speaking and Listening*).
>
> ... listen attentively to stories and poems, and talk about them (*Statement of Attainment, level 2, Speaking and Listening*).
>
> ... hear and share poetry read by the teacher, and each other (*Programme of Study for Reading – general introduction — key stage 1*).
>
> ... hear books, stories and poems read aloud or on radio, tape or television and take part in shared reading experiences with other pupils and the teacher, using texts composed and dictated by the pupils themselves, as well as rhymes, poems, songs and familiar stories from a variety of cultures (*Programme of Study for Reading – detailed provisions for key stage 1*).
>
> ... the reading materials provided should include a range of fiction, non-fiction and poetry (*Programme of Study for Reading – general provisions for key stage 2*).
>
> ... listen and respond to stories, poems and other material read aloud, expressing opinions informed by what has been read (*Statement of Attainmment, level 2, Reading*).
>
> ... demonstrate, in talking about stories and poems, that they are beginning to use inference, deduction and previous reading experience to find and appreciate meanings beyond the literal (*Statement of Attainment, level 3, Reading*).
>
> ... demonstrate in talking about a range of fiction and poetry which

they have read, an ability to explore preferences (*Statement of Attainment, level 4, Reading*).

. . . demonstrate, in talking about fiction, non-fiction, poetry, and other texts that they are developing their own views and can support them by reference to some details in the text (*Statement of Attainment, level 5, Reading*).

Summary

Poetry appears to be emerging from the doldrums. Its growing popularity is reflected in the many new approaches which are being adopted in primary schools. There are more poetry books available now and, in many cases, more opportunities to read them. Knowledge of poetry and poets can be encouraged by many activities, particularly small group discussion. Spoken poetry, often seen as a chore in the past, is being transformed into a useful, stimulating experience.

References

Benton, M. (1978) 'Poetry for children – a neglected art'. *Children's Literature in Education*. Vol. 19, Nos. 3 and 4.

Benton, M. *et al.* (1986) *Young Readers responding to Poems*. Routledge.

Bradley, L. and Bryant, P. E. (1983) 'Categorising sounds and learning to read – a causal connection.' *Nature*. Vol. 301, No. 5899.

Bradley, L. (1987) 'Rhyme recognition and reading and spelling in young children. *Pre-school Preview of Reading Failure*, York Press.

Bradley, L. (1987) 'Early intervention and learning to read – a follow up study.' Paper presented to British Psychological Society, December.

Brownjohn, S. (1980) *Does it have to rhyme*?; (1982) *What rhymes with secret?*; (1989) *The ability to name cats*. Hodder and Stoughton.

Calthrop, K. and Ede, J. (1984) *Not 'Daffodils' Again*. Longman.

Fenwick, G. (1986) 'The Revival of Poetry', *Times Educational Supplement*, 10 October.

Fox, G. and Merrick, B. (1987) '36 things to do with a poem' in Hoffman *et al. Children, Language and Literature*. Open University Press.

Grugeon, D. and Grugeon, E. (1973) *Language and Literature*. Open Univeristy Press.

Rowe, A. (1989) *101 Good Poetry Books*. Language and Information Centre, Reading University.

Styles, M. and Triggs, P. (1988) *Poetry 0–16*. Books for Keeps.

Other useful sources

Balaam, J. and Merrick, B. (1987) *Exploring poetry 5–8*. National Association for the Teaching of English.

Bennet, J. and Chambers, A. (1984) *Poetry for Children*. Thimble Press.
Clancy, D. and Gill, D. (1985) *One potato, two potato*. Macmillan.
Hall, L. (1989) *Poetry for Life. A practical guide to teaching poetry in the primary school*. Cassell.
Reeves, J. (1972) *Understanding Poetry*. Pan.
Sansom, C. (1980) *Acting Rhymes*; (1980) *Counting Rhymes*. A. and C. Black.
Scannell, V. (1987) 'Introducing poetry to young children'. *Children's Literature in Education*, Vol. 18, No. 4.

Useful addresses

Poetry Society, 21 Earls Court Square, London, SW5 9DE (for details of poets in schools).
Book Trust, Book House, 4 East Hill, London SW18 2QE (for details of poets and writers in schools).

Acknowledgements

Daniel, Andrew, Philip, Pat and Peter for their poems.
Frank Maguire for the transcript of small group discussion.

CHAPTER 6

Writing Poetry

By listening to and reading a variety of poems children can be encouraged to create their own. When they do, they are more likely to understand poetry.

There is some cynicism attached to children's poetry, not least by children themselves. Children's poems, particularly in classrooms where they are rare, tend to please teachers. Consequently, a hastily devised verse which requires much less effort than more sustained prose can gain undue praise. Teachers need to be wary of what might be dubbed the 'if in doubt, write a poem' approach. Then there is the fixation with rhyming. Transcripts of discussions about poetry reveal that many children expect that it should rhyme. One reason for this may be that they have not been presented with a wide variety of poems and that the reason for rhyming has not been fully discussed. Popular though they are, Edward Lear's limericks have not helped in this respect. Along with nursery rhymes they are the poems many children are most familiar with. Perhaps they impress the idea of a fixed rhyming pattern too firmly into children's heads.

Where do we start then? It could be with an approach that many teachers might not recognise as having much to do with poetry at all.

Concrete poetry

Sometimes known as shape poetry or calligrams, the amusingly named concrete verse involves experimenting with letters and words – important factors in poetry writing. There is also the implication that words can be made to look like their meanings. Stanley Cook, a versatile poet who has exhibited his concrete poetry, claims that many words in our language already do. 'Pool', 'wave', 'eye' and 'dragon' are words which support this contention. When certain letters are emphasised, the point is reinforced.

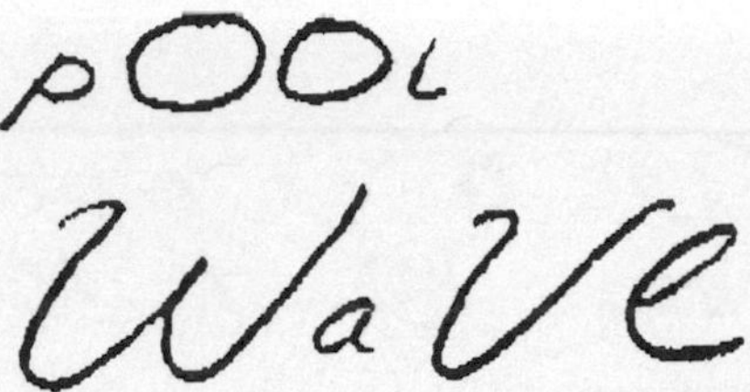

There are no strict rules for concrete poetry. Notice how Stanley Cook arranges the word 'mill' in a powerful way without surrendering meaning (Figure 6.1). Letters do not have to retain their correct position: nor does the exact number of letters needed to be used. For example, the word tree might be made to resemble its meaning by using a single t and a large number of e's and r's. Young children need to have stencilled letters provided for this work, others can make their own shapes or work in pencil, paint or felt pen. This form of poetry

Figure 6.1

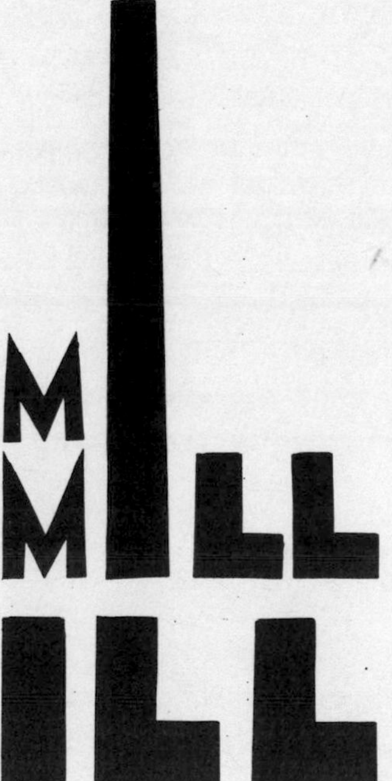

appeals to children throughout the primary school and some very attractive and original results can occur.

There is more than this to concrete verse. A phrase or sentence might be converted,

Wild White Waves
Oranges and lemons

or a pictogram element might be introduced.

The sat on the

More involved is the approach which creates poetic writing in the shape of the key word. Let Karen, aged 10, demonstrate.

What is the mystery
of the funny
question mark?
How
does it
happen?
Did
someone
twist
the long
exclamation mark
so
it
had
a head?
That's
how
they
found out
a new
meaning
to
this
thing.

Do you
under-
stand?

(This is similar in form to Lewis Carroll's 'Fury the Mouse' which occurs in *Alice in Wonderland*).

Finally, a picture of a word might be drawn and the interior completely filled with poetic writing. Let Karen demonstrate again.

Umbrellas are
unusual in many a
way, blue and white twirl
together, round and round and
appear green, etched in their skins
are wiggly little patterns, hard to see
with the naked eye, and a raindrop drops
from a cloud's eye and slips down the damp and
cold
material
and
away
to
become
another
rain-
drop
one
day.

Concrete poetry will always have its detractors but exhibitions of children's attempts are often so original that many adults are converted. It is reassuring to see some of Stanley Cook's concrete poems appearing now in conventional anthologies.

Poetic structure

Exactly what constitutes a poem is subject to a wide number of interpretations. The belief that a poem should scan is probably as strong as the notion that it should rhyme. Whatever approach we take with children, it seems essential that the whole idea of structure should be examined. Take, for example, the limerick. Many junior children are familiar with it and often produce their own versions. But do they know the accepted rules? A limerick is usually four, not five, lines long. The first, second and fourth lines rhyme and the third contains its own double rhyme. If the example of Edward Lear, the foremost of limerick writers, is followed then the last line will contain bizarre and even original invented words. Equipped with this knowledge, children are more likely to write something better than the inevitable lady from Leeds who swallowed a packet of seeds.

Taking the idea of structure further, older juniors might examine the work of William McGonigal, a remarkable poet in many respects. McGonigal's obsession with rhyming often resulted in pure comedy, especially in the later lines of some of his poems. These were extended in length until his quest for a rhyme was successful. Too often, children's poetry is rather like this save that they begin to encounter problems rather earlier. After three or four lines, often of some quality, they begin to struggle as the need to rhyme overcomes meaning and clarity.

By examining various kinds of poetic writing children come to realise that rhyming is not paramount but merely one of many devices which can be used. No one has done more to reinforce this in recent years than Sandy Brownjohn. In a series of low priced and extremely useful books she demonstrates the ideas which she has tried out with children. Some of them, which are really games, can be used with infants. Alliteration, chants, counting rhymes, alphabet rhymes can all be used in this way.

Seven selfish shellfish
saw six swimming seals
sing songs.

(*Andrew, aged 8*)

Words, weird, wonderful, wacky,
Which words will we play with?
Words watching words
In a time warp of W's,
Watchers wishing,
Witches whizzing,
Workman wanting warmth.

(*Karen, aged 10*)

Children can spot the rule here, just as they can in the rather over-worked acrostic.

Hi, I am Helen
Each person has a name
Like mine
Each person has a name
No matter what it is.

(*Helen, aged 8*)

More demanding are syllable count poems such as the haiku, tanka and cinquain forms. Many children tackle these with enthusiasm although some dislike their somewhat constrictive nature. In actual fact, few teachers would be very worried if the three lines of a haiku contained five, eight and six syllables instead of the prescribed five, seven and five.

Some children who have immense difficulty with poetry and writing in general seem to gain confidence by trying out this sort of poetry. Tony, aged 7, wrote very little until, quite suddenly, he produced this statement in haiku form.

> My name is Tony,
> I have green eyes and I live
> In Burleigh Road South.

Later he became bold enough to invent his own form of poetry, four lines each of three syllables. Nobody helped to work it out. It was his own invention.

> The reason
> for a clown
> is to make
> people laugh

Other examples include *Storm* and *Everton*.

> Oh no
> I can see it,
> A storm's here again,
> It's so fierce and far too strong . . .
> thunder
> (*A cinquain by Simon, aged 7*)

> Everton, the best,
> Fifty-nil at Liverpool,
> Everton is great,
> Colin Harvey is the best,
> Everton, the best
> (*A rather optimistic tanka by Daniel, aged 10*)

Using haiku or tanka form some children can create statements of considerable power.

Babies

> A baby is nice,
> If you are looking at it,
> But if you are not,
> If you are taking care of it,
> Well, that's different.
>
> They cry all night long,
> You never get any sleep,
> They wet their nappies,
> And do something even worse,
> Which I won't mention.
>
> You have to feed them,
> Which is not very easy,
> Because they flick it,
> It hits the wall and ceiling,
> But never their mouths.

They try to eat your
        Plants, dried peel or anything,
In fact they are just
        Crying, wetting menaces
Who look very nice.
(*Adam, aged 10*)

I am going there,
To the castle on the hill,
I shall leave tonight.

There is no one here,
I wonder where they could be?
I will just walk in.

Did I see a ghost?
I must have imagined it,
I shall walk straight on.

Could there be a ghost?
I do not know what to think,
Is there a ghost here?

If there is a ghost
There could be vampires as well,
Or could there be traps?

Did that armour move?
Did that picture move also?
Are there several ghosts?

If there is a ghost,
I shall not wait to find out,
I shall exit . . .NOW
(*Gregory, aged 10*)

Poetry can also be used to convey information in an unconventional way. Would Karen's knowledgeable writing have been as attractive or as interesting had she submitted it in prose?

Ladybird Sonnet

The ladybird skitters and flits around
With two hard wing cases on her red back,
One spot, two spot, seven spot, twenty-one,
There is a saying which says the number
Of spots it has is how may times you
Will marry: they eat green aphids most of
The time, then fly off on small grey-black wings,
They have small black heads and two antennae
With which they see and find their way about:
They are minute and they are red, orange
And yellow, they have six black legs and lay
Eggs from which even tinier ones crawl.
They feed the babies on tiny black fly
And in winter the poor things drop dead.
(*Karen, aged 10*)

An equally effective illustration of the same point might be seen in Steven's haiku.

Dolphin's not a fish,
The dancer of the ocean,
Squeaking to people.
(*Steven, aged 9*)

There are seventeen syllables in this poem and just twelve words. It might have been preferable for the strict convention of haiku writing not to be obeyed so that the first line was suffixed with the word 'A'. But this is cavilling. Much more important, consider the amount of information which these twelve words convey.

- Dolphins are mammals.
- They are admired for their acrobatics and grace.
- They have a language which is squeaky to the human ear.
- They can communicate with humans.

There is a good case here for the encouragement of concise writing. Clearly, and contrary to some teachers' opinions, poetry can be an excellent vehicle for this.

Little of the poetry used here actually rhymes. None of these children were instructed either way. They were presented with a number of alternatives and seemed to be more comfortable with those in which rhyming played little part. When they did return to rhyme, it seemed to be more relaxed. Antonia's brief comment might serve as an example.

I would like . . .
to go to the fair
and have lots of ice cream
here and there.
(*Antonia, aged 7*)

Unless the writers demand privacy (and they have every right to) some of their poetry should be published in one form or another. I often take a selection of children's poems and type them up in a booklet form. Spaces are left for illustrations. These do not necessarily have to be done by the poets themselves, although many children would not wish someone else to illustrate their work. Copies are distributed to the writers. Some are also placed in class libraries alongside the work of established poets.

The poems used here to illustrate my points have been written by pupils of junior school age. This is because I have been working with this age range recently. Writing poetry is by no means exclusive to

Figure 6.2

juniors. Stanley Cook has achieved some striking results with infants attempting concrete poetry, and acrostics, alliteration, rhyme and rhythm can all be employed to help very young children to write their own poetry. Collective poems where each pupil contributes a line are also very useful. They might be taped before they are recorded in writing.

Figure 6.3

Lonely
Nowhere to go.
Waiting, watching, wanting.
I've been here before many times.
Heartache.
K. Fielding.

Teachers as poets

Morag Styles has made the apt point that many teachers who request their pupils to write poetry with some frequency would not dream of trying to write it themselves. In Chapter 4 we considered evidence which showed that pupils appreciate teachers who practise what they preach. Furthermore, the National Curriculum requires teachers to write alongside their pupils.

Can teachers be poets? Three very fine poets, Seamus Heaney, Ted Hughes and Charles Causley have been teachers; others include Gareth Owen, John Cunliffe (better known as the creator of Postman Pat) and Wendy Cope. So we have some inspiring examples.

Working with teachers in training is a useful starting point. Some years ago a teacher in Kenyon Calthrop's study reported that in twenty years of teaching she had worked with only one student who had wished to teach poetry. Despite the isolated nature of this observation

I suspect that such occurrences were by no means uncommon. Hopefully they are less frequent today.

Most students are able to create some sort of poetry without too much difficulty. Many of them enjoy the creation of concrete poems and haiku. Some hide behind the anonymity of routine statements about everyday life. Others seem more able to come to terms with their feelings and write confidently about occurrences in students' lives – loneliness, home sickness, falling in and out of love, happiness, fear of teaching practice, success, excitement. Often they place their work alongside that of their pupils, in well produced, word-processed anthologies. There is something very gratifying about seeing a poem by Paula Newall (aged 22) beside those of her pupils, Keith (aged 9) and Denise (aged 10).

Autumn

Across the woodland
The dusky leaves are falling,
Autumn has drawn breath.
(*Paula Newall*)

Figure 6.4

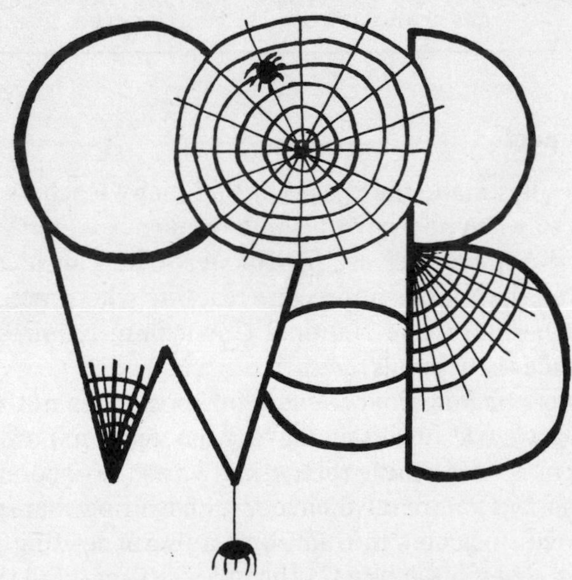

Figure 6.5

Teachers are usually more cautious. Many of them have had similar experiences to my own – no one ever asked them to write poetry at school. Some find it very hard to break away from the idea that poetry has to rhyme. At times this can work to their advantage and they produce narrative poems, cleverly using repetitive phrases and choruses to move the story along. One teacher experienced immense difficulty when trying to write a short story. His alternative, a very acceptable and well illustrated tale in verse, has been much read by infant and younger junior pupils. 'Farmer Bill's Horse and the New Tractor' includes:

'Well done, old Bob,
Cheered Farmer Bill,
'I think I'm going
To need you still.
(*Alan Brewer*)

Many teachers enjoy creating concrete poetry. Unfortunately, 'Cobweb' has been rendered anonymous by the span of time. I hope its creator will recognise it with pride. And the same applies to 'Football'.

A number of the teachers with whom I have worked have had their writing published. Some of their poems have been broadcast: others have appeared in poetry journals and in local newspapers. The following poem was written by a teacher who did not think that she could write creatively – until she tried.

Flight

Stark against an amethyst sky,
    Geese fly,
How do they know, these migrant strings,
    Where to go?
My duck, listening, white neck strains,
    As she deigns
Fastidiously to peck the seed;
    Does she heed?
Does she yearn, as I do, to be free,
    Or need no senseless yearning
Just to be?

(*Joan Campbell*)

Teachers, like their pupils, respect people who practise what they preach. I write poetry myself.

It would be wrong of me to create the impression that because teachers and children write their own poetry, all of it should be shared in one way or another. A number of teachers who have written poetry with me have found that it helps them to come to terms with events in their lives. Some of their poems are deeply personal and are really for their writers rather than for anyone else. They might be shared and understood, usually without comment and certainly without publicity. Gregory, whose poem you have read, did not particularly want a large audience. 'You won't tell them, will you?' he requested to me one day on hearing that I would be visiting his school. I did not. But I wondered if he might like to help Anon who has written some very fine poems indeed.

Poetry writing in the National Curriculum

Before concentrating on the writing of poetry it is worth remembering that teachers are encouraged to write also, although exactly what they write is not stipulated. In the general provisions of the programme of study for Writing this is mentioned as follows:

> (iv) Pupils should see adults writing. Teachers should write alongside pupils, sharing and talking about their writing . . .

In the detailed programme, poetry writing is mentioned with some frequency – on three occasions in key stage 1 and once in key stage 2. For example,

> (iv) play with language, for example by making up jingles, poems, word games, riddles . . .(*key stage 1*)

(5) have opportunities to write poetry (individually, in small groups or as a class) and to experiment with different layouts, rhymes, rhythms, verse structures, and with all kinds of sound effects and verbal play. (*key stage 2*)

Unfortunately these good intentions are not backed up by specific references in the relevant statements of attainment. Not one of these from levels 1 to 5 mentions poetry writing. And it is mentioned only twice, at levels 4 and 5, in the related examples:

> . . . express feelings in forms such as letters, poems, invitations etc. (*level 4*)
>
> . . . draft a story, a script or a poem, a description or a report. (*level 5*)

This is disappointing. Although it is possible to interpret many of the statements of attainment so that they incorporate poetry writing, teachers would have been encouraged by a more positive approach.

Once again, the National Curriculum conveys uncertainty. Despite this lack of direction there is no reason why children should not be helped to write poetry long before they reach level 4 or 5. When it comes to poetry writing it appears that it is up to teachers to shape the National Curriculum rather than vice versa. This is by no means an unhealthy situation. By demonstrating that their pupils can create poems in a variety of forms from an early age they will be doing much to ensure that poetry writing will be accorded more importance in subsequent revisions of the National Curriculum.

Summary

Writing poetry cannot be divorced from the study of poetry in general. The process is cyclical. By reading poetry and talking about it, many children are motivated to make their own attempts. And by writing their own poetry they are more likely to develop a better understanding of the work of more established practitioners.

Very young children can experiment with rhyme, rhythm and alliteration and can attempt simple versions of shape or concrete poetry with some confidence. Later the structure of poetry can be investigated by ways which help children to experiment with a variety of structures as opposed to concentrating solely on rhyme.

The best efforts of both teachers and their pupils should be included in school and class libraries alongside the work of established poets.

References

Brownjohn, S. (1980) *Does it have to rhyme?*; (1982) *What rhymes with secret?*; (1989) *The ability to name cats*. Hodder and Stoughton.

Cook, S. (1975) *Seeing your Meaning: Concrete Poetry in Language and Education*; (1975) *Flowers – 14 Concrete Poems*. Obtainable from Mr Cook at 600 Barnsley Road, Sheffield S5 6HA.

Cook, S. (1984) *Concrete Poems*. Keepsake Press.

Acknowledgements

To Daniel, Karen, Simon, Steven, Andrew, Tony, Gregory, Adam, Helen and Antonia for their poems.

Alan Brewer, Joan Campbell, Keith Fielding, Paula Newall and Denise Sandall for their poems. Stanley Cook for his concrete poem 'Mill'.

Also to the anonymous donors of 'Cobweb' and 'Football'.

CHAPTER 7

Alternative Fiction

Children's experience of fiction is by no means confined to the standardised forms which we all know and recognise. The popularity of comics, for example, is undeniable although some adults are reluctant to accept that such material is literature. Cartoon and pop-up books have been regarded until recently with similar suspicion. At least they are all printed material which is more than can be said for films, audio-tapes and video-tapes, all of which have a place in the teaching of children's literature today.

Controversy still remains about the effects of TV on children's reading. An early study came to the conclusion that the two activities were so different that watching television was unlikely to have much effect on the amount of reading which children do. Whitehead's work appeared to find completely the opposite. The conclusion was that children watch more and more television as they grow older and read less and less. Perhaps the mistake has been to regard the two as rivals. At a time when the book of the film is almost as common as the film of the book, it should be fairly clear that much that children see on the small screen can, in fact, complement written forms of literature. In many ways, it already does. A host of programmes provided for Schools' Television are magnificent and other programmes, such as 'Jackanory' and 'The Book Tower' are well known, established and informative.

It was probably always thus. Perhaps the monks working away at their hand-produced books winced at the crudities of the early printed word. In my infancy listening to the radio (or the wireless as it was called in those days) was often discouraged. Yet listening to 'Children's Hour' helped me to become a confident reader. Children went to the films 'too often'; then as the cinema declined in popularity they watched 'too much television'. Now they probably watch 'too many videos'.

The purpose of this chapter is to explore the potential of these alternative forms of literature and to see how they might be used in a positive way. This is not a case of joining rather than losing. It is an attempt to see what is good, useful and constructive.

Comics

Comics are certainly popular with children. Yet even today many educationists regard them with suspicion. Year after year articles appear in the national and educational press which usually are highly critical of what were once called 'penny dreadfuls'. Usually criticisms are concerned with violence, sexism, racism, slang and an overall deficiency of vocabulary.

It has taken the teaching profession many years to revise its opinions of comics. Many teachers are still by no means convinced of their use. Yet over seventy years ago that enlightened pioneer, A. S. Neill of Summerhill fame, was advocating their use in schools. It is doubtful if many of his colleagues agreed with him. The main strengths of the comic paper, claimed Neill, were brevity and clarity. These might well be at least two reasons for their popularity with children, most of whom prefer to complete their reading material fairly quickly.

As most teachers will know, comics are available in schools. The following conversation which I had with a well known educationist some years ago illustrates that suspicion of comics dies hard.

Educationist	What do you think about comics then?
GF	I like them. They're useful. We should use them in school.
Educationist	But only for wet playtimes.
GF	Why? Children enjoy Asterix the Gaul. There's not much difference between that and the Beano.
Educationist	Ah, but Asterix is a cartoon book.

In almost every primary classroom you will find a store of comics, gathered together for use when the weather is inclement and children are confined to the classroom during break times. If comics are so useful in keeping cooped up children relatively placid, might their wider use be worth examining?

Whether we praise or criticise this kind of material, the fact remains that there is no such thing as a typical comic. Many of them are not even humorous, a point which might seem surprising given the collective term with which we describe them. At primary level children read at least four different types and it is important that the differences which exist between them should be examined. The categories are young children's comics; comics for junior pupils; girls' comics; sports comics for boys.

Comics for young children

These are all very much alike. Even their titles are all fairly similar. For example, over the years *Twinkle*, *Magic*, *Jack and Jill*, *Pippin in Playland*, *Playhour*, *Rupert*, *My Little Pony* and *Postman Pat* have all provided young children with material which does not markedly differ from one comic to the next. The paper is of good quality and the price is not cheap. Two of the current crop, *Postman Pat* and *Rupert*, retail at 40p and 50p respectively. Media characters are often used as an attraction and usually appear on the front page. Apart from those already mentioned, The Wombles, Magic Roundabout characters and Thomas the Tank Engine have all been used in this way. The stories are concerned mainly with domestic situations, fairies and anthropomorphic animals. There is little if any violence and the humour is very gentle.

Much of the written material in these comics occurs beneath the cartoon frames, and even when it is in the occasional speech bubble it is not exclusively in capital letters as is the case in comics for older children. There are often simple games such as spotting hidden objects and unscrambling letters. Overall, the image is one of harmless, rather bland productions to which one can take little exception. They would probably be quite acceptable in most infant classrooms although the general impression is that they are really meant to be read to children by their parents.

As to possible criticisms, there still remains an element of sexism in the current publications. Women still tend to be housebound. And there are not enough multi-ethnic characters. There is, however, little evidence of slang and the number of words is surprisingly high. In a recent issue of *Postman Pat*, for example, there are approximately 800 words. Much of this backs up the contention of Sister Jude, a researcher who came to the conclusion 40 years ago that the vocabulary of comics for young children was rarely harmful.

Comics for junior pupils

Here we probably enter the heartland of children's comics. Once more, the titles are fairly similar but now they are more lively, hinting perhaps at the frenetic activities which are portrayed within their pages. *Whizzer* and *Chips*, *Buster*, *Whoopee*, *Topper* and, of course, *Beano* and *Dandy* are typical examples. Although the artistic presentation of these comics has improved in recent years, the paper is of a poorer quality than that of young children's comics and the prices are cheaper. At present 30p is the top price, with both the *Beano* and the *Dandy* being well below this.

These comics are certainly funny in a slapstick way. There is a great deal of activity going on although little of it is realistic. The characters are almost invariably young and fight a constant war against adult domination. The vast majority of the words are contained in the speech bubbles and usually consist entirely of capital letters. The illustrations are adequate but give the impression of haste, and those cartoons which are coloured are often garish.

Once again, the number of words which these comics contain is deceptive. It is rather like estimating the number of birds in a flock and then actually counting them: the second total is almost always greater. It is very rare for any of these comics to have fewer than 1,000 words in a single copy and nearer to 2,000 is not unusual.

These comics are not without their critics. Probably the main bone of contention is the presence of violence. Almost all of it is of the custard pie variety, being quite impossible in everyday life. Few children read these comics before the age of seven, and by then they are well aware of the differences between fact and fantasy in terms of violence. As Nicholas Tucker claims, it is the very daftness of this kind of violence which pushes children into reading rather different comics as they reach the end of primary education.

As with comics for younger children, there is still a regrettable absence of multi-ethnic characters beyond the token stage. But at least there are now very few examples of blatant prejudice. This was not always the case. Like most other publications, wartime comics were acceptable vehicles of propaganda and scathing references to Wops and Nasties occurred. Adolf Hitler, Hermann Goering and Mussolini were all targets of comic-style humour in the forties. Perhaps in context it is understandable. Of course, they have all long since disappeared along with cannibals with bones through their noses and American Indians whose complete vocabulary consisted of Wah and Ug.

In these comics sexism is rather difficult to pin down. There are often female characters, a fair number of them being principal ones. The gangs are often mixed. For instance The Bash Street Kids in the *Beano* attend a mixed school where the boys by no means dominate the girls. Many cartoons, however, are all male. Few, if any, are exclusively female.

All of these comics contain a considerable number of non-words, but does this really matter? 'Rrip', 'yaroo', 'gnomp' and 'gnahoo' seem harmless enough. And they are far exceeded by the amount of vocabulary which is relevant and at times demanding. Some years ago I examined several copies of *Nutty*, a comic which is now defunct. The following words occurred.

Stranded	Confiscating	Relaxing	Courageous
Tongue	Oriental	Automatic	Assembly
Fossils	Puncture	Vacuum	Concert
Fearsome	Favourite	Wealthy	Reaction
Notorious	Headache	Metronome	Revenge

No debate on comics would be complete without special mention of the *Beano* and the *Dandy*. Comics come and go with surprising rapidity. Even the original version of the *Eagle* comic was not particularly long lived. Yet the *Beano* and the *Dandy* have both existed for more than 50 years. What is their secret? Why have they been so consistently popular? One reason is that they had become established before the war and were allowed to continue during it. Because of this their many strong characters became well known. Desperate Dan has been ever present in the *Dandy* and Dennis the Menace, The Bash Street Kids, and Roger the Dodger of the *Beano* have been about for many years. Whether we like it or not, the *Beano* and the *Dandy* are part of our literary heritage.

Comics for girls

As older children tire of the frantic but unlikely humour of *Whizzer*, *Dandy*, *Buster* and all, the girls move on to comics which are definitely female orientated. *Bunty* is the earliest but *Girl* and *Judy* are fairly similar. Once again, most of the titles are not unalike. In these comics humour has departed. The cartoons are serious stories about girls' schools, often of the boarding variety, ballet, tennis and horse riding. Some of the cartoons are photographed rather than drawn and the emphasis is very much on the teenager.

Sporting comics

Boys stick with the slapstick longer than the girls. When they are ready for a change some of them begin to read comics with a sporting emphasis. Of these, *Roy of the Rovers* is the best known. Once again, humour has gone, there is more vocabulary and the subject material is limited, much of it being concerned with football. Although the plots might be rather stereotyped, these comics are fairly harmless and are certainly in line with older primary boys' interests.

Using comics

The most obvious use to which comics can be put must be reading. Of course, teachers will have accepted much of the reasoning in this chapter so far if comics are accepted in this way. Provided this happens, there seems to be no reason why comics should not take their place alongside other reading material in sessions of Sustained Silent Reading.

Comics, particularly those for juniors, provide useful ways by which direct speech might be understood. Cartoon bubbles invariably contain direct speech and once children realise this their understanding improves. They can then proceed to creating their own speech bubbles. Comprehension is another skill to which comics can be harnessed. Cut the cartoon frames out and request that they should be sequenced. Alternatively, remove the writing beneath the cartoon frames or even delete the speech bubbles and request children to provide their own versions. And, of course, children can create their own cartoons although care should be taken not to demand too much in this respect. A cartoon of three or four frames will be quite enough for most primary pupils: more than that and the exercise becomes too complicated.

The ease with which such exercises can be done reinforces the case for comics to be treated as a useful branch of children's literature. The compilers of comics face a difficult task, a fact which is often obscured by the hurried nature of the art work. In cartoons the message must be conveyed principally by the pictures. Words are added for exact meaning but there must not be too many. Obtaining the right balance requires much skill. Too many words ruin a cartoon. Some years ago a number of cartoon books were published which took for their subjects Shakespeare plays. Much of the original dialogue was used and as a result the speech bubbles became almost as large as the cartoon frames. It did not seem very convincing.

Does writing necessarily have to be lengthy to be good? Is the skill of the cartoonist one which children might use, if only to learn that economic use of prose can be effective? Or, to develop the idea further, might such work reveal the subtle relationship between word and picture? It is interesting to note how the publishers of reading schemes now make extensive use of strategies which at one time were the preserve of comics. Context clues which make use of pictures are more frequent these days, and children's readers are short in order that they can be completed quickly. Clearly comics, in their own way, can be educative. Moreover, many of their characteristics are now being used in other forms of literature.

Cartoon books

Whatever reservations adults might have about comics, cartoon books have come into their own in recent years. Prior to the 1970s there was little or no tradition for material of quality in this country, the exception being the popular Rupert Bear annuals which owed much to the artistic brilliance of the late Arthur Bestall. We relied on imports, some of them excellent. The Tintin books by the Belgian artist Hergé are still popular, although the humour is a little droll for British tastes and some of the content might now be regarded as racist. More attractive were the Asterix books which appeared in this country once it became obvious that Gallic wit and punning could stand translation. Apart from the verbal witticisms, the Asterix books are pure slapstick and in style and illustration are not dissimilar to those giants of the comic world, the *Beano* and the *Dandy*. Another influence came from across the Atlantic. Most of Maurice Sendak's work has little to do with cartoons, but two popular and influential books – *In the Night Kitchen* and *Where the Wild Things Are* – certainly approach cartoon style in their format. *Where the Wild Things Are* was greeted with horror by teachers and librarians when it was introduced to this country because it was thought that its monsters would terrify its young audience. Young children, most of whom enjoy being mildly frightened anyway, were perceptive enough to see that the monsters were benign. Many years after its introduction, most infant classrooms still have a copy.

The obvious popularity of these imports encouraged British artists to take this genre seriously. Roger Hargreaves' *Mr Men* books – which like Sendak's are more cartoon style than cartoon – were attractive to young children, but it was Raymond Briggs whose influence was most profound.

With the arrival of *Father Christmas* the cartoon book in this country was revolutionised. There is little doubt that Briggs's quirky sense of humour assisted in this process. Briggs has a way of turning society on its head. Thus Father Christmas becomes a rather bad-tempered old man, fed up with having to climb down inconvenient chimneys. And the eponymous *Fungus the Bogeyman* lives in a world where scruffiness and filth predominate and cleanliness is eschewed. At times the humour is scatalogical. Adult stomachs need to be strong to cope with Fungus's vulgarities, and not a few teachers have banned *Father Christmas* from their schools because of the small but infamous toilet picture. But above all else, there is the quality of illustration and layout which makes Briggs's books so attractive. The cartoon frames come in all shapes and sizes: there are tiny boxes, quarter pages, quarter double pages and, at least once in every book, a full double page cartoon. The colouring is never harsh and the characters are well drawn. In most cases the stories are communicated with a minimum of words. *The Snowman* is, perhaps, the epitomisation of the cartoonist's art. It tells a story which is clear to children of all ages, not to mention adults, without using a single word.

The important link between words and pictures has already been discussed with particular respect to comics. The message is conveyed mainly by the pictures and supplemented by an economic use of words. Where cartoon books differ from comics is in the quality of the illustrations. Their superiority in this respect can hardly be surprising. It is not that the artists who are employed by the publishers of comics are necessarily an inferior breed, it is simply that they are under relentless pressure to meet deadlines week after week. The better the comic, the harder this is. Practically all of the illustrators of the original *Eagle* comic, perhaps the finest comic ever produced in the United Kingdom, departed fairly quickly. The strain was too great.

Creators of cartoon books work at a by no means leisurely pace. Guy Uderzo, the survivor of the original team which created the Asterix series, is said to work seven days a week for seven months to produce a single book. Briggs takes about two years, Sendak even longer. But there is more time and the deadlines are not so severe. This is reflected in the overall quality of presentation but especially in the quality of the illustrations. With the exception of the *Eagle* no comic has been able to approach the level of art-work which Sendak and Briggs bring to their books. Interestingly, Raymond Briggs contributed a series of cartoons to the Guardian newspaper for a short time. His line drawings were quite crude and this, combined with the absence of colour, made the work unremarkable. Could this have been due also to the time scale which was so different from the one applied to the rest of his work? Since Briggs's emergence in the early seventies, cartoon books in this country have become more popular and more acceptable. Other distinguished artists such as the Ahlbergs and Shirley Hughes have produced work of high quality, and cartoon books are now commonplace. Their future as a reputable genre of children's literature appears to be secure for the time being.

Cartoon books of the right level are often an ideal introduction to literature for many young children. They continue the important link between words and pictures already established by picture books and comics, and help children to become adept at working out the meanings which this combination provides so successfully.

Good cartoon books are no longer the preserve of the young. If *Father Christmas* and *The Snowman* are essentially for children of primary age, then *Fungus the Bogeyman* is for top juniors and younger secondary pupils. *Gentleman Jim* is for young adults and *When the Wind Blows* is really for grown-ups. Cartoon books of quality no longer begin and end with Rupert.

Pop-up books and like materials

These books go back as far as the Victorian era at least. Many fine examples were created in those times. Technology has enabled modern day versions to achieve high levels of ingenuity and inventiveness. Monsters, weight lifters and space rockets leap from the opened pages and tabs can be manipulated to make moving pictures. At a more simple level, flaps and holes are employed to add excitement to the story.

The outstanding creator of pop-up books today is Jan Pienkowski whose *Haunted House* and *Robot* are both magnificent examples of the art. In the former the bats literally rustle as their wings are opened. Less spectacular but just as enjoyable to young children are John Goodall's books, particularly *Lavinia's Cottage*. Eric Carle makes excellent use of the flaps and holes approach, as do the Ahlbergs.

Critics claim that some of these books are little more than gimmicks with little sense of story, acting merely as a showcase for their creators' spectacular art. This is true to some extent. But those which are truly successful are the ones in which the story is more than an excuse for artistic device and where artistry supports a convincing plot.

The popularity of this type of material is undeniable. It promotes an interest in both art and literature but can be expensive. The shelf-life of pop-ups is brief unless their popularity is sheltered by an arrangement that makes their borrowing a privilege rather than an automatic right.

Radio

When radio was more influential than it is today its relationship with children's literature was very strong. 'Children's Hour' (an outstanding programme) did much to encourage children's interest in books. In my childhood many stories came originally via broadcasts. Like many adults, I still remember with great pleasure 'Toytown' with Larry the Lamb, Ernest the Policeman, the Mayor and the irascible Mr Grouser. Such broadcasts have not been lost entirely although 'Children's Hour' has long been a programme of the past. Careful scrutiny of programme details in newspapers and the *Radio Times* will reveal a surprising number of stories to be heard at all sorts of times. Only recently, Alan Bennett was reading a serialised version of *The Wind in the Willows* on Radio 3.

There is also the long established Schools' Radio service. Quite apart from excellent and long standing programmes such as 'Poetry Corner' and 'Living Language', there are a number of others directly related to children's literature. During the present school year the following could all be used in this way.

Let's Join In	Nellie and the Dragon
Let's Make a Story	Listening and Reading
One potato, two potato	Let's Listen
Stories from Listening Corner	Listen
Pictures in Your Mind	Reading Corner

There is a need to be selective. Radio programmes should not be used in isolation. 'Poetry Corner', for instance, could be linked with other poetry work going on in the classroom. Programmes that are particularly useful should be recorded so that they can be used again when appropriate.

Audiotapes and cassettes

This field has developed rapidly in recent years. A large array of tapes is available. It includes material to suit both pre-school and primary school children.

These tapes have a number of advantages. The readers are all experienced, many of them being well known actors or media persons whose names and voices are well known. They include the late Kenneth Williams, Hayley Mills, Glenda Jackson, Richard Baker, Roy Dotrice and Willie Rushton. On some of the tapes other voices are brought in for dialogue and there are sound effects of all kinds, particularly music. The presentation is dramatic. This is absolutely necessary when the competition includes videotapes and live performances. Length varies. There are shortened versions lasting no more than 30 minutes and others which are unabridged and take as long as nine hours to hear completely.

Audiotapes can be used in a number of ways. Whole class sessions are popular when the tapes are short. Serialised versions of the longer ones are sometimes attempted. Most important, tape-banks should be an essential component of school and class libraries and there should be listening corners for pupils to make individual use of taped stories. Ideally, headphone sets should be available for this activity.

Observing children listening to tapes individually, it is possible to notice a different pattern of story listening. The relationship between the child and the unseen teller can become surprisingly personal. Chuckles, objections, murmurs of encouragement, even shouts, all come from children in this situation. Many of them seem to find this relationship a satisfying one. This is not surprising. Many children, particularly those whose reading has yet to really develop, find reading appropriate stories very difficult. By the time they can master them they have outgrown many of these tales. The individual use of story tapes goes some way towards ensuring that these children do not lose out completely.

A number of large publishers now retail audiotapes. They include Collins, Oxford, Puffin and the BBC. Some are enterprising enough to include a copy of the book. Much of this material is also available in bookstores.

Films and television

For many years film makers have recognised the commercial value of young audiences. One of the earliest responses was the Walt Disney version of *Snow White*. Now, such films can be seen frequently. Many children's classics and a variety of other stories have been adapted for the screen. *Oliver Twist*, *Treasure Island*, *Charlotte's Web*, *The Wind in the Willows*, *Watership Down* and *The Railway Children* are but a few examples. First available at the cinema, most of them also occur on the small screen sooner or later.

An interesting question which often arises is which should occur first, viewing or reading? My instinctive guess is that books should be read before the filmed versions are used. Reading leaves more to children's imagination and because of this they are likely to be able to cope with films in a more critical way. When the film is watched first, impressions about characters, especially their appearance, tend to be forced on the watchers. This might make reading a less useful, less pleasant occupation. This does not always apply. So much depends upon quality, and the written and filmed versions rarely match in this respect. It would be surprising if they did. The best match, in my opinion, was *The Railway Children* where both book and film were superb. Occasionally, the film is far superior. *The Last of the Mohicans*, for example, was once a most popular book but it has dated badly, to such an extent that it would be surprising to find it in any primary school today. Yet it made a superb serialised film. This is an example of how some books are best perpetuated in non-written form.

In a recent small scale study, primary school children who had watched a serialised version of *Stig of the Dump* seemed to regard the book and the film as being different enough to allow separate comment. They enjoyed the suspense of the serialisation but wanted to refer to the book in order to understand the story better. Conversely, some of them claimed that the film helped them to understand dialogue which was confusing in the printed version. Clearly, there are no hard and fast rules and it seems fairly certain that this is an area which would benefit from closer study.

Serialised versions of books are obviously produced for television rather than for the cinema. They are usually popular and certainly authors do not object. In some cases a serialised version on television can increase annual sales of a book by as much as fifty per cent. The implication is that television does encourage reading.

Much of this material is not confined to children's television. Newspapers, both local and national, should be scrutinised for advance notice of relevant work. The periodical *Books for Keeps* provides advance notice from time to time. Use should also be made of plays and pantomimes.

We are still none too certain about the relationship between books and film, but there is little doubt that it can be a positive one. It is important that a systematic approach should be adopted. If possible, work should be planned well in advance. At times a film might be the climax of a prolonged topic. Another might be the sparking point for work not yet started.

Children's television offers a number of outstanding programmes outside the confines of Schools' Television. We have already mentioned the long running 'Jackanory' which has made an invaluable contribution to story-telling, and 'The Book Tower' on Yorkshire Television which examines both factual books and fiction in an entertaining way. Schools' Television has the advantage of having both commercial and non-commercial channels, so there is more to choose from than there is on national radio, although in fairness it must be admitted that regional radio also provides useful material, often of a local nature.

Examining what is available for schools on television, one is impressed by the importance which is obviously accorded to myths and legends, particularly to those from other lands, as well as to contemporary children's literature. There is now an interesting tendency to involve the people who write and illustrate books.

Examples of useful TV programmes now available are as follows.

BBC	**ITV**
Storytime	Time for a Story
Words and Pictures	Talk, Write and Read
Look and Read	Middle English
Dragon Trail	
English Time	

As with radio, one has to be selective and link programmes with the general pattern of work in children's literature within a particular school. But the excellent nature of Schools' Television material cannot be doubted.

Videotapes

There is, of course, nothing to prevent films which are televised being videotaped for future use in school. But this section is referring briefly to the commercial tapes available in video shops and stores. The mixture is a curious one. Media characters in animated cartoon films jostle for attention with versions of the classics and some contemporary fiction. Looking through several shelves recently I encountered *Care Bears*, *The Smurfs*, *Yogi Bear*, *Dracula*, *The Wind in the Willows*, *The Count of Monte Cristo*, *Peter Pan* and *Treasure Island*. Perhaps the educational impact of videotapes has yet to be developed. Certainly it does not compare with what is offered on audiotape. Indiscriminate purchases are not recommended. On a more positive note, a commercial company, Weston Woods, has for many years supplied video cassettes at a reasonable price. Their current offerings, mainly for young children, include *Rosie's Walk* by Pat Hutchins, *Moon Man* by Tom Ungerer and *Little Tim and the Brave Sea Captain* by Edward Ardizzone.

Alternative fiction and the National Curriculum

Alternative fiction certainly appears to be regarded as a teaching aid. It is mentioned obliquely in the programmes of study for both Reading, and Speaking and Listening.

> . . . securing responses to visual and aural stimuli
> . . . making use of audio and video recordings as appropriate
> (*Programme of study for Speaking and Listening – general introduction*)
>
> . . . include the use, where appropriate, of audio and/or video recorders, radio, television . . .
> (*Programme of study for Speaking and Listening – general provisions – key stages 2 to 4*)
>
> . . . hear books, stories and poems read aloud or on radio, tape or television . . .
> (*Programme of study for Reading – detailed provisions*)

Unfortunately, there is little in the relevant attainment targets which backs this up.

Teachers who are aware of what is available obviously have a head start. But there is more to alternative fiction than this. Audio and video tapes can be used in a systematic way, being treated not simply as an extra but on a par with conventional approaches to story-telling. With film this is vital: otherwise one is likely to encourage the passive watching which is a feature of so much television viewing. The development of response to literature should be concerned as much with film and tape as with books.

Comics, cartoon books and pop-ups also merit more interest, mainly because they help children to understand that there is far more to fiction than the printed word.

Summary

Alternative fiction is an important part of children's literature. Although many teachers might doubt the value of comics, the case for their inclusion in school libraries is not unreasonable. This could be done at very little extra cost, for it is likely that pupils would be glad to contribute their back copies. Cartoon books represent a natural progression from the comic format and their worth is rarely in doubt. Films, broadcasts, audiotapes and videotapes can be incorporated into the literature programme with little difficulty and can do much to enhance it.

Treated in a systematic way, alternative fiction complements rather than opposes literature.

References

Barker, M. (1989) *Comics – Ideology, Power and the Critics*. University of Manchester Press.

Cooper, M. (1984) 'Televised books and their effect on children's reading', *Use of English*, Spring.

Fenwick, G. (1977) 'Comics – an alternative view', *Reading II*, No. 2, July.

Fenwick, G. (1982) 'Comics and Education', *Bookmark*, No. 9.

Ingham, J. (1982) 'Television viewing and reading habits', *Reading* 16.

Neill, A. (1916) *A Dominie's Log*. Herbert Jenkins.

Sister Jude (1949) 'Six- and seven-year old children's acquaintance with the vocabulary of comics', *Studies in Reading*, Vol. I. University of London Press.

Tucker, N. (1981) *The Child and the Book*. Cambridge University Press.

Whitehead, F. *et al.* (1977) *Children and their Books*. Macmillan.

Useful sources

ITV Schools Programmes, Thames Television, 149 Tottenham Court Road, London W1P 9LL.

BBC Radio and Television, BBC Schools Publications, PO Box 234, Wetherby, West Yorkshire LS23 7EU.

Weston Woods, 14 Friday Street, Henley-on-Thames, Oxfordshire RG9 1AH.

BBC Records, Woodlands, 80 Wood Lane, London W12 0TT.

Collins–Caedmon, 1 Westmead, Farnborough, Hants.

CHAPTER 8

Finding out about Books

> They must have taught me how to read because I was always reading – any old rubbish. Trouble was, they didn't tell me what to read.
>
> (Johnny Speight in 'Johnny Speight and Alf go home', By-line, BBC TV 24 July 1989)

Originally this was to have been the first chapter of this book. It seemed logical: find out about books and the rest should follow. I had forgotten just how complicated book selection has become. Indeed, it is the most difficult problem confronting those who teach children's literature in schools at the present time.

It has been estimated that 5,000 children's books are published annually, and that does not take into account new editions of those already published. Perhaps too many children's books are being published today. Does this matter? After all, the quality of books in terms of presentation and illustration is very high these days. You see very few books which are not visually attractive. This is a far cry from the days when children had to endure library shelves no more than half filled and worn out books often covered in brown paper. Survivors from those days might be entitled to ask what we are worrying about. Yet it does matter what children read in schools. There has to be range and balance. If there is not, then children will not always read what they like or like what they read with any consistency.

Within a primary school there should be ample supplies of

- picture books for young children;
- picture books for older children;
- cartoon books;
- pop-up books;
- poetry;

- comics;
- cassettes, films and videos;
- collections of short stories;
- myths, legends and folklore;
- other fiction.

Most of these categories speak for themselves. Young children are attracted by visual material with not many words and large print. Older children also appreciate picture books, a fact which is sometimes forgotten in classrooms, but they have to be quite sophisticated. Victor Ambrus, John Burningham, Shirley Hughes and Graham Oakley are good examples of illustrators who produce appropriate material in this respect. Children throughout the primary school are attracted by pop-up books and unconventional picture books adorned with interesting holes and flaps. Show this sort of material to most children and you will be killed in the rush. There are cartoon books to suit all ages and the same applies to myths, legends and folklore. And many children prefer collections of stories rather than one long, continuous text. We have already considered the merits of poetry, comics and audio and video cassettes. We are left with what is described on the list as 'other fiction'. This term, in fact, covers that huge body of writing which is conventional children's fiction. It is not necessarily based on oral traditions and relies far more on the written word than most of the other publications mentioned.

Fiction of this kind has to be categorised if a balance of literature is to be achieved in primary schools. Dividing it into genres might appear to be artificial and not always easy. There will inevitably be overlaps but, generally, most primary school pupils are interested in books concerned with

- animals;
- puppet-like creatures;
- home life;
- adventure;
- school life;
- mystery;
- sport and recreation;
- history;
- fantasy;
- science fiction;
- gangs.

Children do not always see their fiction in this light and usually require the various genres of fiction to be pointed out to them before they can express preferences. 'Adventure' might cover most of the others but it is a term which is frequently used to categorise books. 'Puppet-like creatures' embraces fairies, goblins and the like as well as anthropomorphic animals such as Paddington Bear, Pooh Bear and Mr Toad. The expression seems to have been originated by Ivor Leng who thought that such creatures could not really be included within the animal genre. Identifying books by genre was a problem to which Leng gave much thought. How, for example, do you categorise a book with a title like *The Mystery of the Missing Pony*? Should it come under sport and recreation or mystery? Should it, in fact, be in a separate genre specifically for pony stories? Leng suggests that a quick examination of the plot will provide a solution which will be more satisfactory than simply relying on the title.

The first two categories in the list above are the ones which attract young children. Gradually, as their reading improves and their interests widen, they become more versatile.

Although I am not particularly keen to question children about genre, recognition of this form of categorisation is useful. There is probably little need to ask questions such as 'Do you like pony stories?' because sensible record keeping and perceptive observation will provide the answers anyway. What is important is that by providing books of varying genre we go some way towards ensuring that there is a good choice of fiction available in our libraries. Furthermore, such variety is more likely to meet the needs of the whole curriculum rather than the language programme only.

A question of quality

It is agreed that the artistic presentation of books is generally good at the present time, but what about the standard of the writing? Does it matter? In an article written many years ago, the distinguished writer Peter Dickinson argued that children viewed books differently from adults. To children, good books might have more to do with the topic involved or identification with the main character. How many primary pupils, for instance, think that Dennis the Menace behaves in a way which they would like to emulate? According to Dickinson, it does not matter too much what is read just as long as a great deal of reading is being done. I would travel some way along that road but prefer the stand taken by A. J. Jenkinson whose work has already been cited. Jenkinson claimed that children, like adults, read at a variety of levels.

At times they regress to material often read previously with much pleasure. Often they will read the same book over and over. The thirteen-year old who reverts to Enid Blyton is reading in this way. On other occasions, children will read material more in line with their ability and understanding. And at other times they will reach out and surprise themselves and others by tackling something which is challenging in the extreme. Four-year olds have been known, admittedly very occasionally, to read the works of Charles Dickens.

To insist on what we might term 'good' or 'appropriate' books all of the time would lead to boredom and resentment. We should allow for a certain amount of fiction in our libraries which while not necessarily being dross will not be of the highest quality either.

In his outstanding research into children's reading interests, Frank Whitehead categorised books in an interesting and economical way. They were either 'quality' or 'non-quality'. Categorising in this way might seem to present a daunting task requiring complicated criteria, yet it was difficult to quarrel with the way it had been done, and I could identify only one book which I felt had been misplaced: Norman Hunter's book *The Incredible Adventures of Professor Branestawm* is a suitable candidate for the quality list in my opinion.

Teachers would experience little difficulty with this categorisation. A quality book is one that is well written, contains suspense and excitement and has the freshness of originality about it. Here, we should think, is a book which, with luck, will last. Not all books can be like this but we should have as many as possible of them in our libraries; and we should tolerate a goodly amount of the non-quality too.

Authors

Selection by author can be helpful but should be treated with caution. It will appeal to many children. Indeed it is a useful strategy which can encourage an increased awareness of both books and writers. Compiling lists of favourite authors can be most useful in this respect. Since fiction is categorised alphabetically in many libraries, a knowledge of writers is likely to make the task of book selection less difficult.

Reliance on authors rather than books can nevertheless create confusion at times. For instance, the Kingman committee put together a list of writers thought to be suitable for primary school pupils, and one of those mentioned was Oscar Wilde. One has to extract Wilde's fairy stories, and *The Happy Prince* and *The Selfish Giant* from the main body of his work before this selection makes sense. There is some danger that conjuring up names implies that quality and range are consistent. Conversely, this might work to children's advantage. Those who rely too much upon Blyton or Dahl may well come to the conclusion that writers are better on some occasions than on others. This might lead them to widen their horizons.

Children's classics

Here we have a body of fiction which is enduring. Some of it goes back to the nineteenth century or earlier. Antiquity, however, is not a criterion. Books are classics not because they are old but because they are good. There are modern classics. Consider the following:

The Wind in the Willows	Kenneth Grahame
Kidnapped	Robert Louis Stevenson
The Lion, the Witch and the Wardrobe	C. S. Lewis
Watership Down	Richard Adams
Thunder and Lightnings	Jan Mark
Winnie the Pooh	A. A. Milne
The Haunted House	Jan Pienkowski
The Tale of Peter Rabbit	Beatrix Potter
Mr Gumpy's Outing	John Burningham

All are acknowledged classics: among them are lengthy stories, mere snippets, picture books and pop-ups. These books span more than a century. Some of them appeal to the very young, others to older children. All of them are outstanding. Children's classics, it seems, come in all shapes and sizes.

Such books are at the heart of literature and represent the very best of writing and illustration. No matter how many books are published annually, most of the classics survive. Most of them should be in schools.

Multicultural books

Twenty years ago this category would have been given scant attention. Today its importance is readily acknowledged. Many teachers are sensitive about material, usually fairly dated, which might cause offence to ethnic minorities. A number of well known writers have been criticised in this respect, notably Hugh Lofting for his portrayal of African people in Dr Doolittle and H.E. Johns for the apparent xenophobia in his Biggles series. Enid Blyton and, to a lesser extent, Roald Dahl have also been subjected to criticism.

Complete books have been written on this subject and it cannot be tackled comprehensively here. Happily, publishers have been alerted to the problem of prejudice in books and it is unlikely that anything of a highly offensive nature would now be published. The most blatant examples have ceased to exist.

More positively, many good books are available, particularly fairy tales, myths, folklore and legends from all over the world. Books in other categories are, unfortunately, not so readily available. There is a tendency, diminishing now, to concentrate on the home lands of ethnic minorities. This, in most cases, really means the home lands of some primary school pupils' parents or even grandparents. There is still a dearth of books which include ethnic minority characters in a British context. Reading Farrukh Dhondy's books, essentially for pupils of secondary age, I have become convinced that the most effective and authentic writers of this material are likely to come from minority groups themselves. There are not enough of them in evidence at present, although it is only a matter of time before John Agard and Buchi Emecheta are joined by many others.

The most difficult problem is to determine what to do with fiction which is excellent in most respects but unfortunately contains attitudes which are outdated. At one level we might consider several black children in fiction. Is there any difference between Little Black Sambo, Epaminondas, and Petronella Breinburg's more recent Sean? In my opinion, the first two are funny 'peculiar' little black characters who generate mirth at the expense of human dignity (i.e. they are funny because they are black) whereas Sean, in a series of books, possesses a more natural comic spirit.

Attitudes towards books with multicultural themes often change quite suddenly. Uncle Tom in Harriet Beecher Stowe's famous novel was revered for many years for his dignity under severe pressure, for his meekness and understanding in harsh circumstances. Suddenly, this interpretation of his character was no longer acceptable to many people. Today, the expression 'Uncle Tom' has a negative connotation. A more recent book, *The Cay* by Theodore Taylor, received much praise and several awards as an example of racial co-operation. Yet shortly afterwards it was criticised for what was regarded as a condescending attitude towards black people.

The recognition of the existence of multicultural fiction brought with it much negative comment in the early years, and rightly so. It is much more positive to look for good books than criticise the bad ones, mainly because the latter hints, at the very least, at some sort of censorship and this often creates defensive attitudes. Despite the fact that there are not nearly enough of them, it is now the good books on which attention is focused. In the past few years dual language books have been published in recognition of the fact that many of our children use English as their second language.

It seems obvious, although it cannot be said often enough, that this category of books should not be confined to schools with a multicultural population. We are a multicultural society.

Non-sexist books

Again, it is quite impossible to deal with this category in great detail. Like multicultural fiction, it would scarcely have been considered two decades ago. Sexist literature does not seem to inflame opinion in the same way as racially prejudiced material, perhaps because there is a general recognition that attitudes have changed very quickly. Gender stereotyping is less common now but the most striking change has been the recognition that women are less likely to be homebound and are thus able to do many jobs for which they would not at one time have been seriously considered. A title such as *Emily the Engine Driver* cannot be regarded as curious in a society where women qualify as engineers and work on building sites.

Strong female characters in children's literature were in evidence long before the advent of feminism. *The Wizard of Oz* and *The Railway Children* both provide evidence in this respect. We should be looking for books like these as well as the newer ones which reflect recent changes in our society. Once again, we should be accentuating the positive.

Obtaining the balance

So far I have tried to establish the need to have a wide range of reading materials available in schools. If we want to achieve a balance of quality and non-quality books, classics, picture books and the rest, how do we go about it? The following suggestions will assist those who have to make the required choices.

1 *Colleagues*

Within every primary school there is at least one teacher who is extremely knowledgeable about children's fiction. In most schools there are now specific responsibility posts for language development, and that implies that literature must be taken into consideration. Valuable experience should be put to the best use.

2 *Children*

If children's response to literature is encouraged and developed in the ways described in previous chapters then it seems natural that they should have some choice in selecting and recommending books for classrooms. This might be done by discussion or by an examination of the reading records which they have maintained. Children's discrimination is obviously not as sophisticated as that of grown-ups and there are many times in the primary school when the teacher inevitably 'knows best'. Nevertheless, it should be helpful for children to exercise some choice in the books which are provided for them. They might make some selections from a travelling exhibition, they might visit booksellers or they might check out the stock of a public library. And then, some of the books which they appreciate should be ordered.

3 *Librarians*

Knowing about books is part of a librarian's task and teachers should endeavour to tap this useful source of information. Most schools maintain links with the public library service and often obtain block loans from the children's section.

There are several other ways in which libraries can assist schools. First, they can arrange a variety of exhibitions of children's books. For a number of years several public libraries in North Wales and the North of England carried all the children's fiction published during the previous five years. Teachers were invited to make use of these collections. Sadly, this type of service has been cut back. To replace it, some libraries now include exhibitions of books which might be included in the ideal school library.

Another useful approach is the 'Book Chat', which involves librarians visiting schools from time to time, bringing in batches of the latest books which they talk about with the teachers. The books are usually left behind for some time so that they can be perused and their value assessed.

Finally, teachers might adopt a common library procedure which is often known as the 'Book Conference'. Before purchase takes place, librarians read books and then meet to discuss their opinions. Some books will be purchased as soon as possible because of their obvious worth: others will be rejected. Yet others will need a second opinion before a decision is made. Children's books are fairly short and a school staff could carry out an operation like this without too much difficulty. More teachers would probably be involved in book selection and they would become more familiar with what was available. Obviously, books would have to be available from publishers or public libraries for this arrangement to work, but there should not be too many problems in this respect. This is an excellent way to use a Baker day. Many schools have already seized on this opportunity.

4 *Teachers' Centres*

Some centres have frequent displays of books, some of them permanent. They can often be persuaded to organise exhibitions which might be beyond the purse of an individual school. Some issue regular publications in which local teachers review recently published books.

5 *Publishers*

Today's catalogues are works of art. Nevertheless, they are no more than pointers towards what might be useful. No publisher will ever tell you that there is anything inferior in the current catalogue. All the books in the catalogue will appear to be never less than good. Yet to order straight from a catalogue is akin to purchasing blindfold. Most publishers can be persuaded to supply books on approval, particularly through the services of travelling representatives.

6 *Booksellers*

There are immense variations here. Books might be sold in a department store in very much the same way as trousers. Specialist shops are usually more helpful. My favourite is a rambling old place with rickety wooden stairs, high shelves, a coal fire in winter and assistants who are both knowledgeable and helpful. Furthermore, it retails second-hand books. This is a neglected area. Although we want the best for our libraries, that does not necessarily mean that books have to be brand new. After all, books are like cars in this respect, they are only first hand on the day of initial purchase.

7 *The national press*

The Times, *The Sunday Times*, *The Observer*, *The Daily Telegraph*, *The Sunday Telegraph* and *The Guardian* all have a number of book reviews each year specifically for children's literature. So do the Literary and Educational supplements of *The Times*.

8 *Specialist publications*

A number of these provide an immense amount of information about books and their authors. *Books for Keeps*, *Books for your Children*, *Growing Point*, *The School Librarian* and *Puffin Post* all provide this service. *Books for Keeps* is an extremely lively journal which is presented attractively and which reviews books for a number of different age ranges. *Books for your Children* is a rather similar publication but is intended mainly for parents. *The School Librarian*, the journal of The Library Association, contains the most comprehensive reviews. *Growing Point* is a modest yet highly popular journal, now in its 28th year, edited by Margery Fisher, a well known authority on children's literature. The *Puffin Post* is really for children but its articles and details of Puffin books are extremely useful. Teachers must decide for themselves which they prefer, but no staff room should be without at least a couple of these publications. Other publications which do not concentrate on the review of books but which are very useful include two extremely practical journals full of good ideas. These are *Junior Education* and *Child Education*. Others which are rather more theoretical but no less useful in their own way are *Signal*, *Children's Literature in Education*, *Use of English* and *English in Education*.

9 *Specialist books*

Over the years a number of distinguished books have been published which provide an overview of children's literature past and present. The best of these are probably *Children's Books In England* (F. J. H. Darton); *Written for Children* (J. R. Townsend); *Tales out of School* (G. Trease); *Intent upon Reading* (M. Fisher); and *The Oxford Guide to Children's Literature* (H. Carpenter and M. Pritchard).

Darton's book is confined to literature of the nineteenth century. The others extend well beyond this. Most of them are reprinted and updated quite frequently. Townsend's *Written for Children*, for instance, which was first published in 1964, went into another edition two years ago. The most up to date is the *Oxford Guide* which is virtually an encyclopaedia of children's literature. It is useful to consult these books from time to time, particularly if one is worried about neglecting some of the good books from the past.

10 *Research*

Probably the best research of all is the individual teacher's attempts to monitor pupils' interests and preferences. Elsewhere, many investigations have provided information which seems to be obvious. Girls tend to read more fiction than boys and are more catholic in their tastes. They will accept books which might appear to be male-oriented without much objection. Boys, however, are unlikely to read books about ballet, ponies or girls' schools. (Or if they do, they prefer to keep it secret.) Other findings are perhaps less obvious and more useful. The peak reading time in terms of the number of books read has moved down steadily for many years. Now, this peak of reading is occurring at the top end of the primary school rather than in the early years of secondary education.

Although it is not surprising that more able children read challenging material earlier and more often than their less able contemporaries, it is worth remembering that these children still read a very wide range of material, including comics.

Frank Whitehead's research involved 8,000 pupils aged 10, 12 and 14 in 193 primary schools and 188 secondary schools. Perhaps the most striking aspect of this work was the scientific nature of its sampling which, when combined with the large number of pupils involved, provided results which could be reasonably applied to children of the ages mentioned in our education system as a whole. This was probably the first investigation into children's reading interests in this country which made use of a computer. Even so, it was 1977 before the final results were published. Thus, with much of the data being collected in 1971, the findings were somewhat out of date on publication. Furthermore, some doubts have to be expressed about information which depends very much upon asking pupils to complete questionnaires about their reading during the previous four weeks. (This is a formidable task for adults – could you state accurately what you had read during the previous month?) Nevertheless, despite these reservations, there is no doubting the usefulness of Whitehead's work in a number of ways. Children's preferences in terms of authors and quality and non-quality books were clearly shown, as well as somewhat worrying details about the small number of books read by many older children.

This information is still worth examining although after thirteen years the list of popular authors looks rather ancient. There is no mention of Robert Westall, Gene Kemp, Richard Adams, Jan Mark, Shirley Hughes or Raymond Briggs, to mention only a few of the authors one might expect to see in a similar list today. This highlights a glaring need: a similar investigation is long overdue. The great advances in computer science would make the operation both easier and more speedy, and such an investigation could profitably consider the interests of very young children provided that different research techniques were used. It is not unreasonable to expect that a survey into the state of our pupils' reading should occur once every decade. Whitehead himself recommended this, and I am optimistic that such research will commence in the not too distant future.

11 *Book awards*

These play a small but important part in book selection. Perhaps the most prestigious is the Carnegie Medal, awarded annually by the Library Association for an outstanding children's book. The Kate Greenaway Medal, also awarded by the Library Association, is for book illustration. These are the most longstanding awards in this country. The Carnegie Medal dates back to 1936, the Greenaway to 1955.

More recently, the number of awards available has increased significantly. At least ten, including the Library Association awards, seem to be permanent. Some are valuable to authors and their publishers in terms of prestige and publicity. Others, like the Whitbread Award, are worth a substantial amount of hard cash.

Not surprisingly, many of the authors and books selected are well known. Fairly recent winning authors include Margaret Mahy, Roald Dahl, Robert Westall, Gene Kemp, and Janet and Allan Ahlberg. Recent award winning books include *The Jolly Postman*, *The Turbulent Term of Tike Tiler*, *Granny was a Buffer Girl* and *Jack the Treacle Eater*. Established writers such as Lucy Boston, Rosemary Sutcliffe and William Mayne have all been the recipients of one or another awards.

Not all award winners achieve lasting fame. In the early days it seemed as though a writer might be recognised for an outstanding overall contribution to children's literature although the actual book selected was by no means the best example of the author's work. And, not surprisingly, many good books and good authors are never recognised in this way. Nevertheless, award winners are worth noting. *Books for Keeps*, *Signal*, *The School Librarian*, *The Guardian* and *The Times* Literary and Educational Supplements usually contain the relevant information, and *Children's Books of the Year* has a list of the previous year's winners. More detailed lists are available from the Book Trust.

The main awards are:

- The Carnegie Medal for an outstanding children's book.
- The Kate Greenaway Medal for distinguished children's book illustration.
- The Guardian Award for children's fiction.
- The Kurt Maschler Award for excellent integration of text and illustration.
- The Mother Goose Award for the best newcomer to children's book illustration.
- The Children's Book Award for fiction for children up to 14.
- The Whitbread Literary Award for the best novel for children aged over 7.
- The Signal Poetry Award for poetry for children or work promoting it.
- The Other Award for progressive anti-racist, anti-sexist literature.
- The Tir Na-og Award for books written in Welsh or set in Wales.
- The Young Observer Teenage Fiction Award for a teenage novel.

12. *The Book Trust*

Formerly known as the National Book League, The Book Trust is a registered educational charity which aims to maintain and develop the public's interest in books. Within it is another organisation, The Children's Book Foundation, which has the task of influencing the public and the Government about the importance of children's reading.

The Book Trust is particularly useful to schools in two ways. First, it publishes annually *Children's Books of the Year*. The selection of over 300 books in categories ranging from Picture Books to Poetry is the responsibility of Julia Eccleshare who has considerable experience of children's literature in the fields of publishing and journalism. Sifting through the mass of books available is a demanding task and, while the selection is inevitably subjective, examination of the books shows them to be of a high standard. Second, these books have been put together to form a travelling exhibition which can be booked by schools and teachers' centres for approximately one week for a relatively modest fee. There are a number of other travelling exhibitions available, including Early Reading, Picture Books and Story Cassettes. Making use of these exhibitions is an excellent way of actually seeing the books and having a reasonable amount of time to examine them.

Lists, lists, lists

Although all of the information given so far in this chapter is intended to be helpful to teachers, it would be unrealistic to pretend that it might not be overwhelming. Individual schools must work out the best means available to them in the light of their experience and resources. Book lists are useful only up to a certain point. They give useful clues about which books might be suitable, but this information is much more helpful if the actual books can be scrutinised. Schools should try to make as much use as possible of libraries, publishers and travelling exhibitions to ensure that this happens. Then there is the question of time.

Teachers today are subjected to immense pressures. Faced with 1,001 demands it is only natural that they will have to cut corners. In such conditions, some of the suggestions expressed in this chapter might well be asking too much of them. Whether this is so or not, teachers need far more help in selecting books than they are given at present.

Towards a national policy on book selection

Might a National Curriculum imply a national policy towards books? Before readers throw up their hands in alarm, this is not to advocate an approach so uniform that every primary school possesses an identical set of books; or, worse still, that teachers treat literature in a uniform way. Far from it: Floppsey Bunny on Fridays and Wendy Cope on Wednesdays across the nation's primary schools is not something that serious educators would want. But is there a need for a national core of books? Might the best picture books, the best children's classics, the best multicultural books, to name but three categories, be placed in a recommended list?

What I envisage is the careful compilation of a list of the best books, past and present. It would be extensive and schools might be required to select a certain proportion of their stock from its various categories. This approach would combine a core of literature in every school alongside books which were more freely chosen.

Money would be needed for such a scheme; for while many schools already have excellent collections of books, building up a core such as this would be beyond the resources of most, if not all. Once the core had been created, maintaining it and adding to it would be less difficult. Each school would not need to have the same books. They would be free to make their own choice from within the various categories. Yet they would all have an adequate stock of excellent literature which could be supplemented with less enduring material. And, of course, more than lists would be needed. A core of books would require a whole series of travelling or permanent exhibitions, perhaps at least one for every local education authority or public library service.

Consider the benefits which such an approach might bring. Her Majesty's Inspectors would no longer need to bemoan the lack of suitable books in schools, although they would still be able to evaluate how effectively they were being used. Teachers would be free, to some extent, of the massive task of selecting from huge quantities of books. Children would have a well balanced and adequate supply of books available to them.

Who would assume responsibility for this? Mention of the Inspectorate reminds me that for many years the DES had a collection of children's books. It was established in 1949 by Miss F.M. Tann, then Chief Inspector for Primary Education. It was wide ranging, kept up to date and accompanied by a catalogue. Recent enquiries suggest that the Tann list has fallen into a neglect which might be terminal. In view of this it seems unlikely that new initiatives will come directly from the DES.

Why not the Book Trust? Its stated aims seem to make it by far the most likely agency to be able to take on this work. Obviously it would have to be subsidised so that administrators and researchers could be made available for the job. National surveys of children's reading along the lines of the Schools Council investigation already described could be carried out, thus taking pupils' opinions into consideration.

There is, of course, a danger that what might be termed 'The

National Book List' could expand so much that it would become unwieldy or even unworkable. In order to avoid this, books which became outdated could be eliminated and replaced by newer material of good quality. Some books would inevitably go out of print, even if they were on The National Book List.

It is necessary to repeat that this approach should not be thought of as a literary straitjacket. The Kingman report suggested certain authors thought suitable for primary school children. This idea was, quite rightly in my opinion, ignored by the subsequent working party. Devising a National Book List would have to be a gradual process and would require very generous funding.

Perhaps I should simply say, 'I have a dream.' With education still being badly underpriced, that is how it might stay. But if the National Curriculum is to become really effective in terms of the development of children's reading, then the dream should become a reality.

Finding out about books and the National Curriculum

One would not expect to find in the pages of National Curriculum documents direct references to the ways by which children might be presented with a wide range of fiction. But the necessity to do so is implicit. A useful way to conclude this book might be to quote an appropriate section from the general introduction to the programme of study for Reading.

> Reading should include picture books, nursery rhymes, poems, folk tales, myths, legends and other literature which takes account of pupils' linguistic competences and backgrounds. Both boys and girls should experience a wide range of children's literature.

And now, I think, we have come full circle.

References

Carpenter, H. and Pritchard, M. (1984) *The Oxford Guide to Children's Literature*. Oxford University Press.

Darton, F. J. H. (1960) *Children's Books in England*. Cambridge University Press.

Dickinson, P. (1970) 'In defence of rubbish', *Children's Literature in Education*, No. 3.

Eccleshare, J. (1990) *Children's Books of the Year*. Andersen Press.

Fisher, M. (1976) *Intent upon Reading*. Hodder and Stoughton.

Jenkinson, A. J. (1940) *What do Boys and Girls Read?* Methuen.

Leng, I. (1967) *Children in the Library*. University of Wales Press.
Trease, G. (1964) *Tales out of School*. Heinemann.
Townsend, J. R. (1964) *Written for Children*. Kestrel.
Whitehead, F. *et al.* (1977) *Children and their Books*. Macmillan.

Useful periodicals

Books for Keeps, 6 Brightfield Road, Lee, London SE12 8QF.
Books for your Children, Rag Doll Publications, Box 507, Edgbaston, Birmingham B15 3BL.
Child Education, Scholastic Publications Ltd, Marlborough House, Holly Walk, Leamington Spa CV32 4LS.
Children's Literature in Education. IBIS Information Services Ltd, Waterside, Lowbell Lane, Colney, St Albans, Herts AL2 1DX.
English in Education. NATE Office, Birley High School, Fox Lane, Freshville, Sheffield S12 4WY.
Growing Point. Margery Fisher, Ashton Manor, Northants HN 7 2JL.
Junior Education. Scholastic Publications, Westfield Road, Southam, Nr Leamington Spa, Warwickshire CV33 0JH.
School Librarian. Schools Library Association, Lidon Library, Barrington Close, Lidon, Swindon SW3 6HF.
Signal. Thimble Press, Lockwood, Station Road, South Woodchester, Stroud, Gloucs GL5 5EQ.
Use of English. Scottish Academic Press, 33 Montgomery Street, Edinburgh EH7 5JX.

Other useful sources

Elkin, J. (1985) *Children's Books for a Multi-Cultural Society*. Books for Keeps.
Bennet, J. (1980) *Reaching out: stories for readers of 6–8*; (1983) *Learning to read with picture books*. Thimble Press.
Fisher, M. (1986) *Classics for children and young people*. Thimble Press.
Heeks, P. (1981) *Choosing and Using Books in the First School*. Macmillan.
Reed, D. (1988) *101 Good Picture Books*. Language and Reading Centre, Reading University.
Rowe, A. (1989) *101 Good Poetry Books*. Language and Reading Centre, Reading University.
The Book Trust, Book House, 45 East Hill, London SW18 2QE.
Letterbox Library, 8 Bradbury Street, London N16 8JN. (A book club and information service which specialises in non-sexist and multicultural literature.)

Index

(References are to authors of influential texts, principal ideas and sources of information. Authors in reference sections only, books, and authors of children's books listed have been omitted in the interests of space and clarity.)